Mosaics
for the first time®

Mosaics
for the first time®

Reham Aarti Jacobsen

Sterling Publishing Co., Inc.
New York
A Sterling/Chapelle Book

Chapelle, Ltd.

Jo Packham
Sara Toliver
Cindy Stoeckl

Editor: Leslie Farmer
Photography: Kevin Dilley for Hazen Photography
Photo Stylist: Suzy Skadburg
Art Director: Karl Haberstich
Copy Editor: Marilyn Goff
Graphic Illustrator: Kim Taylor
Staff: Kelly Ashkettle, Areta Bingham, Donna Chambers,
    Ray Cornia, Emily Frandsen, Lana Hall, MacKenzie Johnson,
    Susan Jorgensen, Jennifer Luman, Melissa Maynard,
    Barbara Milburn, Lecia Monsen, Desirée Wybrow

Library of Congress Cataloging-in-Publication Data

Jacobsen, Reham Aarti
  Mosaics for the first time / Reham Aarti Jacobsen
    p. cm.
  "A Sterling/Chapelle Book."
  ISBN 1-4027-0635-9
  1. Mosaics—Technique. 2. Handicraft. I. Title.
TT910 .J33 2003
738.5—dc22
                                2003015432

10 9 8 7 6 5 4

Published in paperback in 2005 by Sterling Publishing Co., Inc.
387 Park Avenue South, New York, NY 10016
© 2004 by Reham Aarti Jacobsen
Distributed in Canada by Sterling Publishing
c/o Canadian Manda Group, 165 Dufferin Street,
Toronto, Ontario, Canada M6K 3H6
Distributed in the United Kingdom by GMC Distribution Services,
Castle Place, 166 High Street, Lewes, East Sussex, England BN7 1XU
Distributed in Australia by Capricorn Link (Australia) Pty. Ltd.
P.O. Box 704, Windsor, NSW 2756, Australia

Sterling ISBN-13: 978-1-4027-0635-6 Hardcover
     ISBN-10: 1-4027-0635-9

     ISBN-13: 978-1-4027-2780-1 Paperback
     ISBN-10: 1-4027-2780-1

For information about custom editions, special sales, premium and
corporate purchases, please contact Sterling Special Sales
Department at 800-805-5489 or specialsales@sterlingpub.com.

Write Us

If you have questions or comments, please
contact:
Chapelle, Ltd., Inc.,
P.O. Box 9252, Ogden, UT 84409
(801) 621-2777 • (801) 621-2788 Fax
e-mail: chapelle@chapelleltd.com
web site: chapelleltd.com

Table of Contents

Section 1:
Mosaic Basics—10

Section 2:
Basic Techniques—36

Section 3:
Beyond the Basics—60

Section 4:
The Gallery—94

Introduction

Mosaic art has been around for more than 5,000 years, beginning with the Sumerians in the Middle East and the Aztecs in the Americas. These earlier artists used semiprecious stones (lapis lazuli, onyx, turquoise, etc.), shells, gold, and terra-cotta to decorate their furniture, instruments, and dwellings.

The ancient Greeks began creating mosaics with pebbles of contrasting colors, eventually using smaller and smaller stones to achieve more detail. This gradually led to the practice of cutting small cubes from stone and marble for their mosaics.

The Romans used a much simpler monochromatic style of mosaic to decorate communal areas such as shops, baths, etc., because this style was quicker and less expensive to complete yet still durable and beautiful.

The use of mosaic spread with the Roman Empire. However, as it moved from one area to another, it began to take on the local "flavor" in its design elements, resulting in new and distinct styles that are today easily identifiable by region and/or ethnicity.

The Byzantines were responsible for "lifting" mosaics from the floor to the ceiling, and for pioneering the use of specialized glass, made specifically for mosaics called "smalti." Christian artists would later take advantage of both of these evolutions to decorate their places of worship with immense and spectacular representations of biblical subjects and scenes.

Islamic artists were also adept at working with mosaics. When viewing an Islamic mosaic, you will notice the absence of human representation as Islam forbids it. Instead, you see a profusion of geometric and plant-like designs with a liberal dose of calligraphy. These design elements are indicative of the purpose of Islamic art, which is to inspire awe and contemplation of the eternal.

Today, new materials have become widely available that are easier to work with and a lot less expensive. Mosaic has become more of a "creative" art form and not just a decorative one. It is also earth-friendly, in that it recycles items that might otherwise be discarded. Almost anyone with a sense of imagination and creativity can create a beautiful and long-lasting work of mosaic art.

How to use this book

Mosaics for the first time® gives you all the basic information you will need to get started with mosaics.

It is important to remember that mosaic is an ancient art form that has spread all over the world. As such, there are many different opinions on techniques, styles, bases, etc. Do not think of this book as a blueprint; rather think of it as a foundation on which to build your own mosaicking technique.

Everyone eventually settles into a "rhythm" with mosaics—you develop your own personal style. You favor certain adhesives, tesserae, and bases over others . . . you experiment. There are so many ways to express yourself in art; do not be limited by tradition. Be safe and read labels, but, have fun!

Use this book as a starting point and do not be afraid to do things differently; you might become a mosaic pioneer! Always consider the pieces that did not turn out the way you had planned as a good lesson and keep going. You will be amazed how often today's mistake becomes tomorrow's technique.

Also, the projects in this book are used for one of three reasons: to try a technique, to experiment with tesserae, or to familiarize you with tools and materials. I will try to help with little tips about substitutions, but you should feel free, in fact you are encouraged, to try any changes you are inspired to make.

Section 1: Mosaic Basics will familiarize you with the terms,

techniques, and tools you will need to get started. Please read through all the basic components of mosaic (tesserae, bases, adhesives, grout, and safety), then you'll be able to assess your needs in regards to tools. If you do not recognize a word, check the Glossary of Terms on page 109. Section 2: Basic Techniques will take you through some simple projects so you can apply what you have learned in section one. In turn, Section 3: Beyond the Basics combines some of the techniques you have learned for more advanced projects. Finally, in Section 4: The Gallery, you will get a glimpse of what is possible in this art form by viewing some inspiring pieces that have been done by a few talented professional mosaicists.

Section 1: mosaic basics

Tesserae

Tessera (singular) literally means one square of material used in a mosaic. This one square forms the foundation of a mosaic for it is the individual piece, when combined with others and placed in a particular pattern, that makes up the whole. Recently, tessera has taken on a more general connotation and currently refers to any and all pieces that are used to make up the mosaic "picture."

The following information will teach you about the more common types of tesserae (plural) used in mosaics.

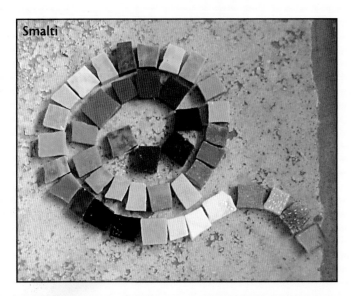

Smalti

Smalti

Designed specifically for mosaics, smalti is made by pouring molten glass into oblong- or disc-shaped (*pizze*) slabs and allowing it to cool slowly, or anneal. The slabs are then cut into pieces. For many generations, smalti has been produced by glassmakers in Venice, Italy, using closely guarded techniques and recipes to achieve the brilliant colors and various opacities that make smalti so attractive to mosaicists.

Glassmakers are able to produce metallic smalti by "sandwiching" real metal leaf between layers of glass. Gold, silver, copper, and gold alloy are the most commonly used. You will find that gold leaf is often placed between layers of dark green, and silver is placed between layers of dark blue to enhance these colors.

Smalti filati is made by pulling the molten glass into threads or rods and cutting it into tiny pieces. Smalti filati is used to make "micro mosaics."

Smalti is generally used in the creation of decorative pieces. The same characteristics that give smalti its unique look (uneven texture and small visible bubbles), make it unsuitable for floors or other surfaces that require an even or flat surface. Grouting will also ruin the look of smalti; most artists use the self-grouting method with smalti.

Smalti Assessment
- Suitable for: Decorative pieces that do not require a level surface
- Cost: Expensive, more so for metallic
- Cutting/Shaping: Wheel glass cutter/nipper, tile nippers, hammer/hardi (a small anvil)
- Availability: On-line, in mixed bags or single colors
- Colors: All, metallic
- Grout: Self-grout
- Sizes: Approximately ½" square; smalti *filati* is approximately 1mm square
- Sold: By the pound, kilo, or slab (rare)

Tile

Tile boasts many qualities that make it ideal for mosaicking. It comes in a variety of shapes and sizes. It also comes in beautiful colors in both glazed (shiny) and unglazed (matte) finishes; it is readily available and relatively inexpensive.

A good way to build up a collection of tiles is to buy closeout pieces, discontinued pieces, remnants, or samples that are available at flooring and hardware stores. However, be aware that this may not be the best way to acquire tiles for every project as you may find that you do not have enough of a particular type or color that is required to complete your mosaic. When calculating a project, always plan carefully and allow for waste and for pieces that may get broken.

Different tiles are made for different applications. Each type of tile is classified by specific characteristics that determine where and how it should be used. Be certain to assess your needs before choosing tile for a project. For example, does it need to be frostproof, nonslip, or

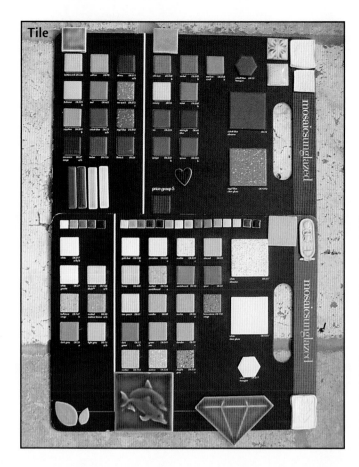

Tile

Tile Assessment
- Suitable for: Just about anything
- Cost: Inexpensive to very expensive
- Cutting/Shaping: Tile nippers, hammer/hardi, tile saw
- Availability: Widely available
- Colors: Earth tones—all colors (glazed)
- Grout: Groutable
- Sizes: 1/4" square to 12" square; unlimited
- Sold: By the sheet, by the box, individually, or loose in a bag

Tile Tips
Always do a few test cuts/breaks on tiles you may want to buy in bulk as some tiles have a tendency to break unevenly or even crumble. Glazes also have a tendency to chip.

Glazed tiles are usually white with the glaze over the top only; unglazed tiles are colored all the way through.

Always seal unglazed tiles and stone to keep them from staining.

hard-wearing? You will be better prepared to make your selection after studying the following rating systems, used by tile manufacturers:

Ability to Withstand Abrasion
- Class I: Walls only
- Class II: Very light foot traffic
- Class III: Medium residential use
- Class IV: Heavy residential use
- Class V: Commercial, durable, stain-resistant

Water Absorption/vitrification
- Nonvitreous: 7%+; prone to stains even when sealed; not suitable for wet areas or heavy traffic
- Semivitreous: 3%–7%; can be sealed, indoor, minimal outdoor, available in frostproof
- Vitreous: 0.5%–3%; okay for wet, high-traffic, or outdoor/cold climate
- Impervious: Below .05%; i.e. porcelain; very hard, stain-resistant, does not require sealing, withstands use in wet and freezing conditions

Stone

Stone often falls under the tile heading as the two materials are often packaged and used in the same manner. One appealing aspect of stone is that it can be purchased in uncut slabs or large pieces. However, it requires the use of stronger tools than would be used for tile (Refer to Cutting Stone on page 30). It also comes in smaller sizes or cubes, which are a bit more expensive.

Stone

The most common stone used in mosaics is marble, but slate, limestone, and others make great tesserae, too.

Stained Glass

With all the colors and textures available, stained glass is a wonderful material for mosaics; it can be manipulated in many ways and used in many interesting variations.

The only downside to working with glass is the potential for injury; it must be handled carefully and safely.

Stained Glass

Stained Glass Assessment
- Suitable for: Tables, decorative, limited functional
- Cost: Inexpensive to very expensive
- Cutting/Shaping: Easy with practice; glass cutter, wheel glass cutter/nipper
- Availability: Glass suppliers, on-line
- Colors: Clear, opaque, flat, textured, iridescent, mottled, multicolored, all colors
- Grout: Groutable
- Sizes: From sheets several feet square to hand-cut $1/2$" squares or scraps
- Sold: By the sheet in varying sizes, or in remnants, strips, cut squares, or scraps

Stained Glass Tip
Glass comes in different thicknesses, so if you want or need a piece to be of uniform finish, make certain all of your glass thicknesses match up. You can also use the indirect, or reverse, method (Refer to Indirect/ Reverse Method on pages 30–31).

Clear glass/Marbles

You can produce unlimited visual effects with clear glass tesserae by applying one of the following types of media either onto your base or onto the back side of the tesserae. You can see some of these effects in the project and gallery sections.

Clear glass/marbles

Using Paper with Clear Glass/Marbles
If you have a picture or a pattern that you would like to put under glass, there are two ways to do this; each produces a very different look.

In the first method, you attach a picture or piece of patterned paper onto the base, then mosaic clear glass tesserae over the paper. The picture or pattern remains intact as it is simply sandwiched between the base and the tesserae.

In the second technique, you attach the back side of clear glass tesserae directly onto the paper, let it dry, then trim the paper close to the edges of the tesserae. The picture or pattern is no longer whole, but in pieces.

Using Stickers with Clear Glass/Marbles
You can easily incorporate any design you might find on stickers into your mosaic. Simply adhere the stickers onto the base, then mosaic clear glass tesserae over them.

Note: Measure stickers and tesserae for optimal placement.

Using Paint with Clear Glass/Marbles
Paint is a wonderful way to achieve the exact color you want for your mosaic. Apply paint onto the surface, then

adhere clear glass tesserae over the paint. Use any paint you like, but remember that your adhesive will be between the paint and the glass so avoid applying it too thickly. Make certain the surface is clean before painting it.

Using Glitter with Clear Glass/Marbles
Glitter lends a subtle metallic effect to your mosaic. Apply glitter in a clear liquid acrylic form onto the surface, then adhere clear glass tesserae over it. Although glitter is slightly thicker, it should be treated the same as paint.

Note: Paint and glitter both can be applied directly onto the back side of glass tesserae. However, you must be careful when breaking or cutting not to scratch any off.

Using Gold Leaf with Clear Glass/Marbles

For a rich metallic look, try applying gold leaf onto a section of your base, then adhering transparent (clear or colored) glass tesserae over it.

Now that you can purchase colored mirror, textured mirror, and van Gogh (mottled mirror), the possibilities seem endless.

Mirror Assessment
- Suitable for: Decorative and limited functional (not recommended for floors)
- Cost: Inexpensive, colors are a little more expensive
- Cutting/Shaping: Easy with practice; glass cutter, wheel glass cutter/nipper
- Availability: Glass suppliers, on-line
- Colors: Clear or amber readily available, colors are usually mail order
- Grout: Groutable, but use a light touch to avoid scratching the mirror
- Sizes: From sheets several feet square to hand-cut $1/2$" squares or scraps
- Sold: By the sheet, or in cut shapes, strips, or squares

Mirror Tip
When attaching mirror, always use 100% silicone or a special adhesive, or mastic, designed for attaching mirrors, as regular adhesives will ruin the silvering on the back of your mirror.

Mirror
We are all familiar with mirrors, and it does not take a lot of imagination to see how it can spice up a mosaic to use a few pieces of mirror here and there. It is also quite striking to see a three-dimensional piece covered entirely in mirror.

China/Crockery
China, porcelain, and earthenware are all suitable for mosaics; they can be used sparingly for effect or en mass for a dramatic flair. All the pieces, including handles, lids, spouts, etc., can be used for fun variations.

Mirror

China/Crockery

China/Crockery Assessment
- Suitable for: Decorative, limited functional
- Cost: Inexpensive (sometimes even free) to expensive
- Cutting/Shaping: Wheel glass cutter/nipper, mallet
- Availability: Readily available
- Colors: Unlimited
- Grout: Groutable, but use a light touch to avoid scratching the design
- Sizes: Various
- Sold: As dinnerware in various shapes and sizes

Vitreous Tile

These are the small colorful glass tiles most commonly used to line swimming pools. They come in a variety of colors and are very durable and uniform in size. They can be used on floors, walls, counters, and decorative pieces.

They have a flat surface and a textured surface. They are usually placed texture side down for better grip, but with stronger adhesives that are now available, the texture side can be used uppermost to create a different effect.

Vitreous Tile

Vitreous Tile Assessment
- Suitable for: Almost anything
- Cost: Reasonable, based on the color
- Cutting/Shaping: Easy; tile nippers, wheel glass cutter/nipper
- Availability: Tile suppliers, on-line
- Colors: All regular to metallic
- Grout: Groutable
- Sizes: $1/4$" square, $3/4$" square
- Sold: By the sheet in a single color, by the pound in a single color, or loose in mixed colors

Vitreous Tile Tip
Remember, these are made of glass, so take precautions and be careful when cutting.

Found Objects

In this category you will find beads, buttons, marbles, shells, pebbles, toys, various food items, and almost anything you can imagine varnishing and gluing down.

Found Objects

Found Objects Assessment
- Suitable for: Usually only decorative, some exceptions
- Cost: Inexpensive (sometimes even free) to expensive
- Cutting/Shaping: Various, depending on item material
- Availability: Various
- Colors: Various
- Grout: Self-grouting; test for other methods
- Sizes: Various
- Sold: Various or found/adapted

Andamento

Andamento refers to the "flow" of the tesserae, or the way you arrange your background in relation to your focal point. It is the backbone of your mosaic and has been described as the mosaic equivalent of the brush stroke.

To achieve different looks, you will usually choose an opus for your focal point, or central picture/design, a contrasting opus for the background, and sometimes a third opus for a border.

Opus Circumactum

This is the name for a circular- or fan-shaped pattern. It is important when using this opus to make certain that the curves mirror each other; if the proportions vary, the imbalance will pull the eye away from the effect and ruin the finished look.

Opus Musivum

In this pattern you outline the focal point, then continue to outline the outline, over and over until you fill in the whole background—this gives a very lively look.

Opus Palladianum

Irregularly cut or broken tesserae are laid out in a "crazy paving" style—the trick to creating a nice effect is to keep the spaces relatively equal between the tesserae. This is a great way to use up bits and pieces of tesserae. However, avoid using too many different sizes, colors, patterns, or textures or it loses its charm.

Opus Regulatum

The tesserae is laid out in a grid. This pattern is very plain but has a dramatic look when used properly.

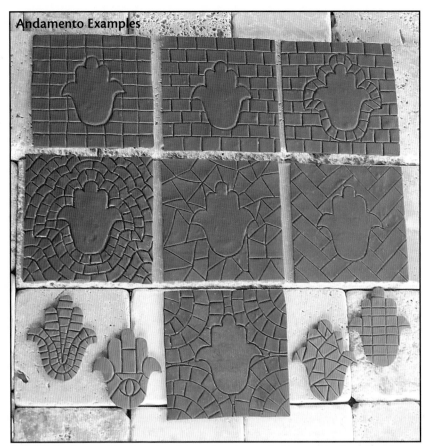

Andamento Examples

Top left: Background in Opus Regulatum. **Top center:** Background in Opus Tessellatum. **Top right:** Background in Opus Vermiculatum. **Middle left:** Background in Opus Musivum. **Middle center:** Back-ground in Opus Palladianum. **Middle right:** Background in Opus Spicatum. **Bottom left:** Focal point in Opus Musivum and Opus Tessellatum. **Bottom center:** Background in Opus Sectile. **Bottom right:** Focal point in Opus Palladianum and Opus Regulatum.

Opus Sectile

This technique is more common among stained glass artists. This opus uses tesserae pieces that are cut individually into shapes that are specifically fitted to each other.

Opus Spicatum

This pattern yields a weave done in the herringbone effect. This is not the easiest choice to work with as a background; it may be a little distracting if your focal point is not well defined.

Opus Tessellatum

The rows of tesserae are laid out in a staggered way, similar to a brickwork design. In this pattern, it is essential that the pieces do not match up or the effect is ruined.

Opus Vermiculatum

The main characteristic of this pattern is that you outline your focal point or design with only one row and then complete rest of the background using Opus Regulatum or Tessellatum or any other contrasting opus.

In the example shown at left, the hand, which is the focal point, or central motif, was done in Opus Palladianum, while the background was done in Opus Tessellatum. The contrast highlights the difference between the two.

Pique assiette

This style of mosaic is better suited for recycling old china or tiles. Basically, you choose a base and cover it with randomly sized and colored pieces, then grout. There is no need to plan a layout or work with measurements and drawings.

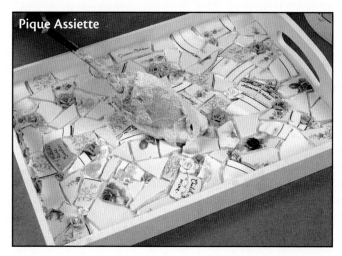

Pique Assiette

This lively incarnation of mosaic is often referred to as "memory ware/jugs," "whatnot," "bits-and-pieces mosaic," or "shardware." The actual name for this style comes from the French term "picassiete" which translates to "stolen plate," "broken plate," or "plate stealer." Moreover, the word "pique" means "crazy" and alludes to the randomness of the style. "Pique assiette," currently the most com-

monly used name for the style, means "scrounger." All of these "colorful" terms were used to describe one Raymond Edouard Isidore, who lived in Chartes, France. Mr. Isidore began collecting shards in 1938 from a field near his home. He then used them, some would say compulsively, to decorate every surface, inside and out of his home and garden. At the time, the neighbors were apparently less than pleased by this obsession, but today approximately 30,000 visitors per year flock to "La Maison Picassiette."

Some mosaicists enjoy using the pique assiette style in a hybridized form, organizing the tesserae to create "quilt-like" designs rather than sticking with the random look typically associated with the pure form.

In either form, pique assiette is a wonderful way to "recycle" beautiful heirlooms that may have met with an unfortunate end. It is an art form found in many cultures around the world and may have some common ancestry with the African tradition of decorating gravesites with the deceased person's "treasures." I have heard it said, and I quite agree, "Pique assiette is where all broken things want to go when they die."

Bases

You can create a mosaic on almost any flat or three-dimensional surface as long as it has been properly prepared. First, it must be sealed to prevent the tesserae from falling off over time. Then it must be "keyed" to give it a "tooth" to aid the grip between the base and tesserae.

Bases

Wood

The most commonly used woods are plywood, MDF (Medium Density Fiberboard), and hardboard. Hardboard works best for intricate cutouts; however, it must be sealed completely (even the edges) so it does not warp. Marine-grade MDF should be used for outdoor applications. Both are available in various thicknesses. The rule of thumb is, "the larger your piece, the thicker the wood must be to keep it from warping under pressure." Use the following as a guide:

$^1/_8$" thick for a project of 18" or less
$^1/_2$" thick for a project up to 36"
$^3/_4$" thick for a project larger than 36"

Keying a Wood Surface
To "key" a wood surface, score it with a hacksaw or a box cutter; the scoring need not be deep—just roughen it a bit.

Sealing a Wood Surface
Dilute PVA adhesive 1:1 with water and brush onto the wood surface to seal it.

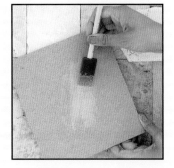

Sanding a Wood Surface
You can also use sand-paper to roughen the surface. Wipe down the sanded base with a clean dry cloth to remove dust. Seal the surface with diluted PVA as described above or with a spray sealant.

Backerboard

Made specifically for tile, backerboard is an excellent choice for mosaics that must be water-resistant, as it remains rigid when wet. It is a bit more expensive, and comes in two types: cement-based panels (require a saw to cut) and lightweight panels of cement with fiberglass mesh (only need a razor to score and cut). Both are available in various thicknesses.

Concrete

Use a concrete base only when dry and in perfect repair. Minor defects may be fixable with a leveling compound. However, do not try to disguise a problem, as it will only make it worse.

Glass

Make certain your glass base is clean and dry. Remove any residue by going over it once with denatured alcohol.

Silicone is an excellent adhesive to use on glass, but take care to minimize air bubbles that may result when placing the tesserae. Clear or semiclear stained-glass tesserae work wonderfully on a glass base as the combination allows light to shine through. Although it is a little time consuming, it is a good idea to make certain the adhesive covers the entire back side of each tessera for a more finished look.

Mesh

Fiber netting, scrim, gauze, and wire mesh are all names you will encounter when choosing a mesh backing. Mesh is useful for creating a slight even curve in a mosaic. It can be cut into any shape and is available in sheets or rolls.

Mesh also provides a way to do an entire mosaic or parts of a mosaic at a location other than the final site. Upon completion, the mosaic (or its parts) can be carefully transported to the final site and permanently attached with epoxy or cement.

Walls/Floors

You will need to make certain the wall is strong enough to hold the final mosaic; when in doubt, consult a professional. As with concrete, when utilizing plaster or painted walls, make certain any existing finishes are sound and keyed. If you decide to use new materials, use cement-based backerboard. When working on an outside wall or stone, use a sand or cement level to create a good bond. Wood floors must be plywood reinforced.

Terra-cotta

Terra-cotta needs to be sealed before adhering any tesserae. Make certain to seal your grout, especially lighter colors, to avoid water damage that may occur with use or as a result of being outdoors.

Papier-mâché/ Cardboard

These paper-based materials must be sealed to prevent the moisture in the adhesive or the grout from damaging them beyond repair.

Metal

Keying a Metal Surface

To "key" a metal surface, use a rough grade of sandpaper or steel wool.

Make certain to wipe down all surfaces that have been keyed with a clean dry cloth before adhering tesserae, as keying a surface will leave small flakes or particles that will interfere with the adhesive grip between the tesserae and the base.

Use a multipurpose adhesive when attaching tesserae onto a metal base, as it will give you a much better bond.

Adhesives

There are many different types of adhesives that can be used for attaching tesserae onto a base. Each has its own set of characteristics that determines how and where it can best be applied. The following adhesives are most often used for creating mosaics.

Adhesives

Cement-based Adhesive

Used in: Direct method
Characteristics: Available in premixed or powdered form, economical, can be colored with additives, available in fast- and slow-setting formulas, requires water cleanup while still moist.

Note: The premixed form tends to dry out in its container.

Epoxy

Used in: Direct method

Characteristics: Available in gel or liquid form, suitable for outdoor and wet applications, strong adhesive, two-part mixing may be messy and time consuming, available in fast- and slow-setting formulas, causes strong fumes, requires use in ventilated area.

EVA – Ethylene Vinyl Acetate

Used in: Direct method

Characteristics: Water-resistant version of PVA, but not waterproof. Suitable for use in areas that may get wet, but not for use in pieces that will be submerged regularly.

Gum Adhesive (Gum Arabic, Gum Mucilage)

Used in: Indirect method

Characteristics: Expensive, more difficult to remove than PVA/Paste, ideal for pieces that must be transported, unsuitable for outdoor or wet applications.

Mastic

Used in: Direct method

Characteristics: Paste, available in premixed form, economical, latex- or petrochemical-based, not as strong as cement-based adhesive, for use in dry, low-traffic areas.

Multipurpose Adhesive

Used in: Direct method

Characteristics: Strong adhesive, available in some basic colors, can be colored with additives, almost all are paintable, thick enough for three-dimensional or vertical applications, read labels for indoor/outdoor and wet compatibility.

PVA – Polyvinyl Acetate

Used in: Indirect method

Characteristics: Liquid, dries clear, requires water cleanup, unsuitable for outdoor or wet applications. PVA adhesive is also used as a sealer for porous mosaic bases such as hardboard, terra-cotta, and papier-mâché. When diluted 1:1 with water and brushed onto the base surface, it gives a good tooth to help the tesserae grip better.

Silicone

Used in: Direct method

Characteristics: Available in gel or thick adhesive form, works well on almost any surface, thick enough for use on three-dimensional or vertical applications, available in clear, white, and almond in small tubes—other colors available for use with caulking gun, expands and contracts with weather conditions, dries to a rubbery finish, not paintable, use with mirrors.

Wallpaper Paste

Used in: Indirect method

Characteristics: Inexpensive, available in powdered or liquid form, requires water cleanup, unsuitable for outdoor or wet applications.

Grout

Grout is the mortar that fills the spaces between the attached tesserae. It is an extra source of strength to the finished mosaic. More importantly, it is the element that pulls your mosaic together visually—it is quite amazing how different your piece will look once it is grouted.

Grout

There are two basic types of grout: cement-based and epoxy-based. Both are available in either sanded and non-sanded formulas.

Sanded vs. Nonsanded Grout

The common use for nonsanded grout is for filling spaces less than $\frac{1}{16}$" wide, while sanded grout is used in wider spaces. However, even for these smaller spaces it is not necessary to use nonsanded grout. In fact, most artists prefer the finished look of sanded grout and use it on all their pieces regardless of the space between the tesserae. Both sanded and nonsanded grouts are available in many colors and can also be colored with additives.

Note: Use a light touch when grouting over china and mirrors with sanded grout. Avoid rubbing too hard when spreading the grout and when cleaning up, as you can scratch the mirror or damage the china pattern.

Cement-based Grout

This is the most commonly used grout. Often, you can find cement-based grout containing powdered polymer or liquid latex additives, which give it increased strength and resilience.

Epoxy-based Grout

Epoxy-based grout is resistant to chemicals, stains, water, and mildew and does not require sealing. It is, however, more expensive and difficult to work with and can take 2–7 days to cure. When dry, it has a dense, slick-looking finish that may not be suitable for "earthy" or rustic applications. It requires special safety precautions, application, and finishing. If it is not cleaned off the tile quickly and as directed by the manufacturer, it is very difficult to correct.

Using epoxy-based grout takes practice. Try it out on a small test piece first before attempting to use it on a large piece.

Note: Due to the level of difficulty involved in working with this type of grout and because this book is for the first-time mosaicist, none of the projects use epoxy-based grout. However, this information is included here to give you a broad understanding of the grouts that are available.

Grout Color

Grout color in creative or decorative mosaics is a personal choice. Each yields a different visual and emotional effect.

Black Grout
Black tends to make the tesserae seem more vivid and makes the piece "pop."

White Grout
White has the opposite effect of "mellowing" the piece.

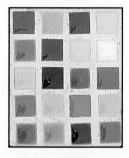

Gray Grout
Gray blends the colors in the piece together.

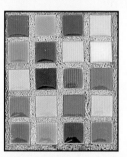

Colored Grout
Using a contrasting color can give a piece a "zany," fun, or more playful look.

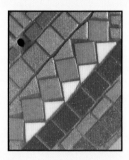

Mixing Grout Colors
Grout is available in many different colors and shades. However, if you need to mix two or more shades of grout to get a lighter, darker, or even totally new color, the best way to do this is to "sift" the powders together using a designated flour sifter.

Mixing Grout with Acrylic Paint

For most of the projects, I suggest using acrylic paint to color your grout. "Why?" you might ask. Simple: it is more cost effective and colorful to buy white grout and color it as needed.

Setting up a work area

Not everyone has the space available to set up a permanent work area. So, when you need to set up a temporary work area, it is a good idea to cover your work surface with paper or, preferably, plastic (a trash bag taped tightly to the table will do). Select a room that has a hard floor—not carpet. Make certain to cut tesserae in a location away from people, pets, and food. Cutting into a large cardboard box will help contain the waste pieces. When grouting, cover up your floor area as grout has a way of getting everywhere.

Have a bucket/bowl of water on hand for washing grout off tools, gloves, or skin. Simply dip in water and wash off. When you have finished grouting, let the water stand until it is mostly clear. The grout will settle in the bottom and you can gently pour off the water. Then tap the sides of the bucket/bowl to loosen the deposit of grout so you can dump it in the trash.

Tools

Before you rush out and buy everything on the following lists, you should know that they are provided mainly to give an overview of tools that you may use while creating a mosaic. Some of these tools are nice to have, but not always essential. You will find that a particular tool may be absolutely vital when working on one mosaic project and completely unnecessary for another. The essential items, or those that should be included as part of your starter set, are highlighted in bold type.

Safety Tools

Safety Tools

- Purchase **rubber gloves** that fit well and have a good durable build. A few extra dollars spent here will save time and help you avoid aggravation while grouting.

- An **air-filter mask** is essential for respiratory protection when working with "mix your own" adhesives, grout, and concrete.

- As with the rubber gloves, it is a good idea to "splurge" on the higher end (around $12) **goggles** or **safety glasses**. When you are selecting your goggles, keep in mind that if you do not like them because of their bulkiness or awkwardness, you will be less likely to wear them. It is imperative that you wear goggles every time you cut tesserae—it only takes one stray shard of glass in the eye to cause serious damage.

- If you get grout on your hands (from a hole in your glove, etc.), rinse them in apple cider vinegar. It will neutralize the chemicals and prevent damage to your skin.

- Vinyl gloves are good to have when working with solvents and spray paints (not shown).

Drawing & Design Tools

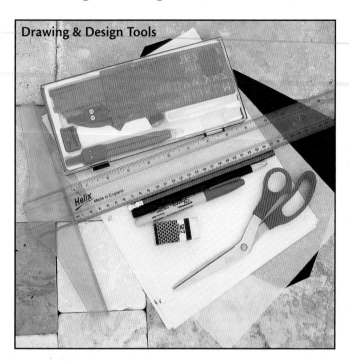

Drawing & Design Tools

• A **geometry set** (compass, protractor, set-square, ruler) is useful for drawing designs and measuring accurately.

• **Pencils, erasers, felt pens,** and **permanent markers** will be necessary at any given time as you work out the design of your mosaic.

• A **T-square** is used to ensure 90˚ angles and to help you measure and draw straight lines.

• Carbon paper, tracing paper, graph paper, and drawing paper can be used to transfer mosaic designs or pictures.

• Templates can be used if you are uncomfortable with your freehand skills. There are almost unlimited templates available that would be suitable for use in mosaic design.

• A pair of craft scissors are useful for cutting paper or template materials.

Drawing & Design Tools Tip
To keep your tools on hand and organized, dedicate a tackle box, a rubber container, or a drawer in a roll-away cart for their storage.

Surface Preparation Tools

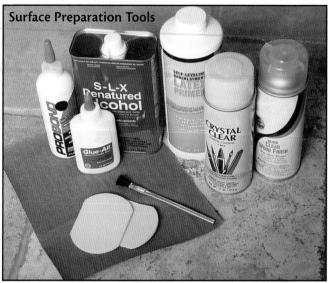

Surface Preparation Tools

• **PVA** or **EVA adhesive** and an **old brush** are necessary for sealing porous surfaces before attaching tesserae.

• A **hacksaw, box cutter, craft knife,** or **rough-grit sandpaper** can be used to key wood or metal surfaces.

• Latex primer (self-leveling) will help correct a surface that is not quite level.

• Denatured alcohol and a clean cloth are used to remove any residue from glass.

Cutting Tools

Cutting Tools

- A **tile nipper** is invaluable for cutting and shaping tile.

- A **wheel glass cutter/nipper** is used to cut and shape glass, smalti, china, and more. This is an indispensable and versatile tool.

- A **cork-backed metal ruler** is used with a glass cutter to score tesserae. The cork prevents the ruler from scratching the tesserae while you cut.

- A glass cutter is used to score straight or curved lines.

- A tile scorer/cutter scores a line on the glass or tile and then helps you "break" it.

- A tile cutter is used for cutting larger tiles. This tool makes quick work out of cutting several strips or small squares.

- Running pliers help break glass when your strips are too small or thin to break by hand.

- A mosaic hammer or a masonry hammer has a sharp end for breaking tesserae and a flat end that can be used with a chisel.

- A chisel is used with a hammer to break stone or tile.

Attaching Tools

Attaching Tools

- An **adhesive spreader** is used to apply an even layer of adhesive.

- **Disposable brushes** also are used to spread adhesive.

- A **multipurpose adhesive** can be used to attach tesserae onto many surfaces.

- A **100% silicone sealant/adhesive** is used to attach mirrors and works well with glass. It is also thick enough to use with three-dimensional or vertical applications, as it keeps the tesserae from sliding.

- Mastic is a setting adhesive that works well for tile. It is available in indoor- and outdoor-compatible formulas, but is not appropriate for all surfaces.

- Heavy welding compound is an epoxy adhesive. It is very strong—use sparingly. This material is available at auto supply stores.

- PVA adhesive is used to attach tesserae onto brown paper when working in the indirect, or reverse, method.

- Premixed grout/adhesive is for use when dealing with tesserae that must be self-grouted.

Grouting Tools

Grouting Tools

Note: All food-oriented tools must be "dedicated" once used for grouting.

- A **bowl** is used for mixing grout.

- A **mixer** is used to stir/mix grout.

- A **float** is used to spread grout.

- A **water container** is used for cleanup (not shown).

- **Clean cloth rags** are used for wiping down and buffing finished piece (not shown). Soft cotton works best.

- A **large trash can** is used for disposing of old grout and other unusable items (not shown).

- **Sponges** are used to wipe off excess grout.

- A grout additive is used when more resistance is required in the mosaic.

- A pointing trowel is used to spread grout into smaller spaces between tesserae.

- Disposable artist-pallet knives work well in very small spaces to spread grout.

- A squeegee is used to spread grout across a large surface such as a floor.

- Old toothbrushes or vegetable brushes are used for clearing away grout and defining details.

Finishing Tools

Finishing Tools

- A **grout sealer** is used to extend the life of your mosaic.

- A **permanent marking pen** is used to sign your art.

- **Spray** or **brush-on acrylic paint** is used for unmosaicked surfaces.

- Picture-hanging hardware is used when you intend to hang your mosaic.

- Adhesive putty or a heavy welding compound can be used to attach hanging hardware to the back side of the base when nails are prohibitive.

Extra Tools

- A cutting system (e.g. Morton®) is useful if you cut large quantities of glass. This tool is usually available from stained-glass suppliers.

- A hammer and hardi (small anvil) are used for stone and smalti cutting. These tools can often be found at stone masonry stores.

- A benchtop grinder or multipurpose tool with a grinding wheel attachment is valuable for smoothing rough edges. This tool is available at stained-glass suppliers or hardware stores.

- A tile stone is a rectangular stone that works as a file to smooth edges and shape tesserae. This tool works well with tile, stone, and china.

- Colored pencils are used for drawing out layouts. (It helps to draw out your picture in color.)

Laying out a mosaic

Q & A

Before you lay out a mosaic, you should ask yourself a few key questions:

- What is the mosaic's purpose?
- Is the mosaic decorative or functional?
- Will the mosaic be permanently placed or movable?
- What style will you use to complete the mosaic—traditional, abstract, or modern?

If, for example, you would like to make a clock to hang on the kitchen wall, it will be functional, moveable, and possibly abstract in design. Because it is functional, be careful with how you lay it out—clock hands must glide smoothly above the surface, so its design should be as uniform as possible. Since the mosaic will hang on the wall, make certain it is a suitable weight for the wall; if it is too heavy, either scale down the project or reinforce the wall. When selecting the tesserae and grout, keep in mind the theme or color of the kitchen. Make certain to choose an appropriate base and adhesive. Because you will be moving the mosaic, plan on sealing the grout and edges so the grout will not slough off or crumble when touched. For an abstract design, start sketching or hunting for layout ideas. Planning ahead eliminates many potential problems that may arise during the mosaicking process.

Planning the Layout

One of the most common ways to layout a mosaic is with a motif or picture in the center, then a background, and finally a border. Use the background to frame the central motif as you would use a mat board to frame a picture, then use your border as you would use a picture frame. Choose an andamento to complement the central motif.

Laying Out a Mosaic

Draw out your design on paper. A rough sketch is a good start, but for best results use exact measurements in your drawing. With a full-scale drawing you will be able to work out any problems ahead of time. Some mosaicists use colored pencils to complete the drawing, working out all their color schemes as well as their measurements beforehand. If a particular piece is not coming together the way you anticipated, try changing measurements or colors.

Layout Tips
Do not hesitate to use a freehand drawing for your layout design.

When using found art, photocopies are great. Use carbon paper to transfer a photocopy onto your base.

You can use designs from all types of sources such as fabric and wallpaper. You can use an entire picture or merely focus on a small portion of the picture and expand or enlarge that part.

Use a subtle or plain background to bring your central motif to the foreground.

Avoid mosaicking edges. Mosaicked edges are weak and do not hold up well to wear. If you are not comfortable grouting the edges, simply frame the piece.

Be flexible when planning out a mosaic; sometimes the mosaic lays itself out despite what you plan. Just go with it and see where it takes you.

Cutting tesserae

Whether you choose to use a cutter or nippers, it is the pressure of squeezing the tesserae between the "jaws" of the tool that cuts or breaks it into pieces. With practice you can control this breaking to achieve shapes. One basic difference to remember: with a tile nipper, only $1/8$" of the jaws of the tool should be on the tesserae. With a wheel glass cutter/nipper, you place the cutting wheels in the center of the line you want to cut.

Cutting Glass

Cutting Glass with a Glass Cutter

1. To cut straight lines, use a cork-backed metal ruler (cork protects the glass from being scratched) and a glass cutter. Hold the tools firmly. Use the glass cutter to score, or scratch, a line across the surface of the glass by pulling it once along one edge of the ruler.

2. Hold the glass with one hand on either side of the scored line and snap the glass by pushing upward with your fingers against your thumbs.

Note: When using a glass cutter, never go over a score line twice as this can cause problems when you are making the break—make certain of your cut the first time.

Using Running Pliers

If you are cutting thin strips you will have to use running pliers to snap the glass. Place the line on the pliers over the scored line and press firmly. The glass will snap. Do not position the jaws of the tool more than ⅛" onto the glass.

Cutting Glass with a Wheel Glass Cutter/Nipper

If you want a more casual look, or you are a good judge of size, you can use the wheel glass cutter/nipper to cut squares from your strips of glass. Simply place the cutting wheels in the center of the strip and squeeze.

Cutting Squares & Rectangles

To cut a square smaller, first cut the square in half, making two rectangles. Then cut the rectangles in half to make squares.

Cutting Circles

To make circles, use a technique called "nibbling," where you use the wheel glass cutter/nipper to take "small bites" away from the edges until you have a round shape.

Cutting Triangles

To make triangles, cut a glass square diagonally from corner to corner.

Cutting Random Shapes

To cut random pieces of glass, you can tilt your wrist to the left or right to achieve different curves or points to a break.

Cutting Glass Tip

Do not cut glass when it is very cold. Warm it in the sun or near a space heater for a cleaner break.

Cutting Tile

Cutting Tile with Tile Nippers

As with pliers or a wheel glass cutter/nipper, position the tile nippers no more than $\frac{1}{8}$" onto the tesserae when making a cut. To cut triangles, do the same, but position the nippers at the corners.

Cutting Shapes with Tile Nippers

To cut shapes, use the nibbling technique to nip away the edges of the tile with the nippers. Nip only to the outside of the shape as you can always cut more off. If you cut into the shape and get too much, you cannot undo it.

Smoothing Tile Edges

After cutting shapes, use a small tile stone to smooth the edges. The stone works just like a file. Make certain that you always file in one direction.

Cutting Tile with a Tile Cutter

1. Place the tile in the cutter, flush with the top edge. Hold the tile with one hand as you score the top by pulling the handle and dragging the scorer across the tile surface.

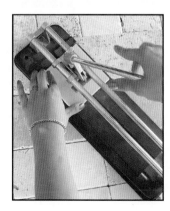

2. Return the handle to the starting position. This will remove the scorer from the surface and position the break piece. Firmly pull straight down; the tile will snap.

Note: The tile should remain in the same position the entire time and, as with glass cutting, only score a line once.

Cutting China/Crockery

Using the "Safety Smash"

To break china or crockery dinnerware into random pieces, use the "safety smash."

1. Place your piece between the layers of a folded towel.

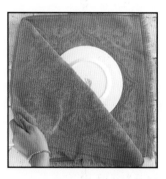

2. Smash with a mallet or hit gently with a hammer.

3. Be aware that all these pieces will have sharp edges, so be careful and watch for small slivers and shards.

Cutting China/Crockery with a Wheel Glass Cutter/Nipper

You can also use a wheel glass cutter/nipper just as with glass. However, china does not always break predictably, so be prepared for the possibility of your cut going awry.

Cutting China/Crockery Tip
If you are having trouble with curved pieces lying flat, cut them smaller; the curve will be less apparent.

Cutting Vitreous Tile

To cut glass tile, use a wheel glass cutter/nipper as you would for cutting glass. Tile nippers, unless they are very sharp, can crush glass tile.

Cutting Smalti

To cut smalti, use a wheel glass cutter/nipper for more control and a cleaner cut.

Note: The traditional way to cut smalti is with a hammer and hardi.

Cutting Stone

Lay your stone on the work surface. Use either a chisel and hammer or the sharp end of a mason's hammer to strike the piece; this will cause the break.

Attaching Tesserae

Direct Method

Direct method simply means attaching the tesserae directly onto your base. The direct method works for most mosaics. It is fairly straightforward and easy to do.

Applying a Bead of Adhesive

To apply a bead of adhesive means to squeeze a line of adhesive from a tube or canister onto the base.

Buttering the Adhesive

Buttering means to spread adhesive onto the tesserae or base.

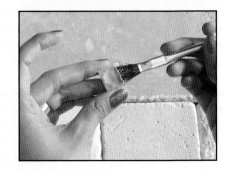

Indirect/Reverse Method

By contrast, the indirect, or reverse, method is a bit more difficult to do. It requires you to lay out your mosaic upside down on a temporary surface, then transfer it onto its final base or location. If you need or want a totally flat, uniform surface, the indirect/reverse method is the best method to use.

The traditional way to do an indirect/reverse mosaic is to draw or transfer your picture in reverse onto brown paper. Attach your tesserae, face down, onto the drawing with a 1:1 solution of PVA (water-soluble glue) and water. Allow the glue to dry. Spread adhesive onto your perma-

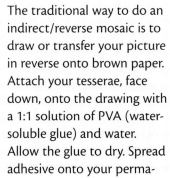

nent base, then "flip" the design over and attach the back side of the tesserae onto the base (the brown paper is now uppermost). Allow the mosaic to set. Dampen the brown paper to break down the water-soluble glue and peel it off to reveal your design. You are then ready to grout the mosaic.

Double-reverse Method

When you are working with tesserae that have a different color back from what you see on the front, such as ceramic tiles, you may wish to use clear contact paper to work the double-reverse method.

In this method, you lay out your mosaic on a picture as in the direct method, then attach the contact paper onto the top, flip, and cover with another piece of contact paper.

The advantage of using contact paper is that you are able to look at your picture to check the progress of the design—just be careful when flipping back and forth. Additionally, you need not use a glue-and-water solution to attach the tesserae onto the paper since it is already sticky.

The best way to flip is to "sandwich" the piece between two pieces of wood, then flip over and remove the top piece of wood.

Note: When your mosaic must be perfectly flat for its application such as on a tabletop, countertop, or floor, use the double-reverse method.

Grouting

Grouting with Cement-based Sanded Grout

1. Pour the determined amount of powdered grout into a dedicated mixing bowl (one cup per square foot is an average amount).

Note: It is okay to have a little more than you need as it can be a problem to have too little and need to mix more, especially when custom-mixing a color.

2. Following the manufacturer's directions, add water or grout additive, stirring in a little at a time until the mixture is similar to the consistency of mayonnaise or sour cream.

3. Mix well, making certain to scrape the bottom and sides of the mixing bowl.

4. Allow the grout to "slake" before spreading it onto your piece. Slaking means allowing the grout mixture to sit for approximately 15 minutes to give all the polymers, latex, or other strengthening agents in the mixture sufficient opportunity to blend, ensuring the best possible grout finish for your piece.

5. Spoon a "glob" of grout onto your mosaic. While wearing gloves, use your hands, a float, a trowel, or other tool to spread the grout. Make certain to work in a crosshatch pattern: working left to right, top to bottom, then right to left, bottom to top. The point is to fill all the spaces in your mosaic with grout, leaving no gaps.

6. Allow the grout to set for approximately 10–15 minutes.

7. With a damp, well-wrung sponge, wipe down the mosaic. The object is not necessarily to clean it, but to remove most of the excess grout from the tesserae.

8. Allow the mosaic to set again for approximately 30 minutes, then do a quick wipe-down with an old rag or paper towel. If the excess grout wipes from the

tesserae easily, it is dry enough to do a first wipe-down; if it smudges all over, allow it to set another 30 minutes and try again.

9. When the piece is thoroughly dry, wipe it down again and buff it to a shine with a clean cloth.

10. If you choose to seal the mosaic, follow the manufacturer's directions on the sealant.

Grouting an Unframed Edge

When you finish grouting a mosaic with an unframed edge, run a very thin layer of residual grout along the outside edge. Seal the edge with a thin layer of multipurpose paintable adhesive sealant.

Grouting a Three-dimensional Object

When you are grouting three-dimensional found objects such as beads or ceramic flowers, gently use your fingers or a paintbrush to work the grout around the objects' edges to avoid damaging them or burying them.

Grouting Tip

If you have a time constraint and are rushing a project (sometimes it is necessary, but avoid it if possible), you can mix a stiffer grout by adding less water—the consistency of peanut butter.

Grouting with Cement-based Nonsanded Grout

The technique for grouting with nonsanded grout is essentially the same; however, the drying time is faster.

Nonsanded grout tends to develop more holes as it dries so watch it carefully. If you see these "pinholes" developing, apply more grout to the piece to fill in the holes.

Grouting with Epoxy-based Grout

If, after you are comfortable with the techniques provided in this book, you would like to use an epoxy-based grout, follow the manufacturer's directions and remember to try it out on a small mosaic piece first, as epoxy-based grout is a little more difficult to work with than cement-based grouts.

Grouting with an Alternative Grout

An alternative grout is anything used to fill the spaces between the tesserae that is not traditional cement-based or epoxy-based grout. You could use this technique, for example, if you would like to use a delicate type of tesserae that will not withstand the traditional grouting process. Simply apply a thick layer of adhesive over the entire base, quickly place your tesserae, and sprinkle the entire piece with a fine material such as glitter or tiny beads. The fine material will stick to the exposed adhesive and fill in the spaces between the tesserae, giving it a "grouted" appearance.

Note: When using an alternative grout, the trick is to work quickly, attaching the tesserae before the adhesive dries out.

Troubleshooting

There are a few mistakes that are quite common when you are learning to mosaic. I have listed those that I come across most often or that I have done myself. There are some mistakes that can be fixed and others that cannot. Although some pieces simply cannot be saved when mistakes are made, there is always something to be learned from the experience.

Mistake #1—Poor Choice of Grout Color

When in doubt, start light. If you cannot decide what color to grout a piece, go for the lightest of your choices; you can always grout over it with a darker color (but usually only once).

You can also try this trick: get a spray bottle, dilute acrylic paint in your choice of color (one part paint to at least six parts water), and spray it over your piece. Quickly wipe the tesserae clean. Make certain to get all your grout lines, and do not get it too wet.

Mistake #2—Colors are Too Similar

Your mosaic has too many similar colors, and no definite look. This happens when you use too many same-tone tesserae. Your picture gets lost and it looks muddled. Unfortunately, there is no fix for this one. You will have to scrap the project and try again.

Mistake #3—Damaged Found Objects

Grout can ruin a found object that is not sealed well or properly. Grout can erode the finish and cloud up a piece such as a seashell or button. One way to correct this is with a touch of paint or even a little nail polish. Make certain that there is barely any paint/polish on the brush, and apply gently over the object. Repeat, if necessary.

Mistake #4— Buried Object

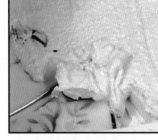

You use a three-dimensional object and it gets lost during grouting. Allow the grout to dry, but not cure completely—an hour or so should do it. Then use a dental tool or toothpick to dig out the excess grout from around and within the details of a object. Use an old toothbrush to clean it. Touch it up if necessary. This process is a little time consuming, but may save the piece.

Note: Use a paintbrush to spread grout around the object.

Mistake #5— Missing Piece

If, during the grouting process, a piece falls out, simply clean it off, leave the spot ungrouted, and reapply it after you have finished grouting. Save some of your grout in a sealed can, jar, or resealable plastic bag so you can grout the piece in later. Saving the grout instead of remixing a new batch will insure an exact color match.

Finishing the piece

To give your mosaic a finished look, as well as protect it from wear or damage, there are a few final steps that follow grouting.

Buff It

Using a soft dry cloth, rub down your mosaic surface to remove any film or residue left over from the grout.

Note: This does not apply to unglazed tile.

When buffing a mosaic that has a mirror, wipe gently as the grout can scratch the surface. When cleaning the mirror itself, spray cleaner on the cloth—not the mirror—and wipe the mirror only so as not to damage the grout.

Finish the Edges

After grouting, you can finish, or "frame," a piece by nailing a strip of metal or gluing moulding (e.g. a picture frame) around the edges.

If you choose to leave the edges unframed, make certain you seal the grout edges with a heavy-duty adhesive or recommended sealant.

Seal the Grout

Unless you used a grout additive, it is always advisable to seal a finished piece to protect it from staining and to seal porous stone or tile. Standard grout sealer, regardless of brand, will work. Make certain to read labels to ensure the sealer is appropriate for your project.

Paint It

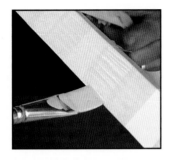

Paint the edges, back, and other unmosaicked parts of your piece to give it a finished look. Match the paint to the grout color or use a complementary color.

Attach a Hanger

If it is a hanging piece, be certain to match the hanging hardware to the weight and needs of your piece. Measure carefully before attaching the hanging hardware, otherwise your piece will hang wrong.

Sign It

No piece of art is complete without the artist's signature. Remember to use a permanent marker.

Safety Reminders

• Make certain to read and follow all project instructions and manufacturer's directions carefully and completely. Be aware that each product will behave in its own unique way.

• Always remember to wear goggles or safety glasses when cutting tesserae. The pressure of breaking can cause pieces to fly at awkward angles, possibly hitting you in the face.

• Wear an air-filter mask when working with dry materials like mix-your-own grout, adhesive mastic, or cement. Dust from these products can cause long-term damage to your respiratory system.

• Always wear good-quality rubber gloves when grouting. The harsh chemicals found in grout will eat away the skin on your hands with prolonged exposure. If you do get grout on your hands, rinse them with apple cider vinegar to neutralize the chemicals, then make certain to wash with soap and water.

• Be careful when working with cut tesserae; a lot of the materials will have sharp edges after cutting.

• Work in a well-ventilated area. Fumes and dust from adhesives and grout can be very harmful to you or other people/pets around your work area.

• Keep children and pets away from your work area. Tesserae are serious choking hazards; and small sharp glass shards from breaking can cause injuries.

• Make certain you are working with clean and well-maintained tools. If a tool looks like it might be broken, discard it and replace it with a new one. Try to keep tools in a designated place in your work area for easy access when you need them. Tools, such as bowls and spoons, should be dedicated to your craft once they are used for mosaicking.

• Always try to clean up your work area after you have finished a project. A clean, organized work area will help to minimize mishaps. It also makes it more enjoyable to begin a new project without having to deal with an old mess first.

Finding the things you will need

Hardware/Lumber Store

Go aisle by aisle; you will find all sorts of things that would make great bases or tesserae. Also, check out different adhesives every once in a while—manufacturer's come out with new types all the time. Keep in mind that most hardware superstores will do simple wood cuts for you; they also offer a selection of precut smaller pieces.

Craft Store

This project-oriented source is also a good place to browse; the beauty of mosaic art is the ability to recognize and use many items that you would normally overlook.

Dollar Store

Here, you can find affordable grouting supplies like bowls, sponges, and spatulas.

Salvage Store

This is a terrific source for finding old tile, bases (furniture), and interesting found objects.

Flea Market

Here is another wonderful source for finding dishes and bases.

On-line

You can find everything you need for mosaics on-line. You may find yourself ordering supplies from half way around the world, but it will be worth the wait. See Acknowledgments on pages 110–111 for a list of websites.

Specialty Store

For hard-to-find tools and materials, you will have to go to specialty stores such as stained-glass suppliers, tile outlets, frame shops, etc.

Thrift Store

A second-hand store is a great place to find old dishes and an assortment of unusual bases.

See Acknowledgments for more ideas about where you can find mosaicking supplies and tools.

Section 2: basic techniques

How do I use the self-grout technique?

What you need to get started:

Tesserae
Smalti, rainbow colors

Additional Supplies
Acrylic paint to match frame
    color
Multipurpose adhesive
Paintbrush
Picture frame, 5" x 7"

The self-grout technique is achieved by laying down a bead of adhesive on the surface and pressing the tesserae into the adhesive, leaving little or no gap between the pieces.

Smalti Picture Frame

Here's how:

Note: This piece does not require a surface prep because we use a very strong adhesive and relatively light tesserae. This piece will not come into heavy use, so this adhesive grip should suffice.

1. Apply a bead of multipurpose adhesive along the front side of frame, centered within its width.

2. Press the smalti into the adhesive in a rainbow pattern along the frame, with as small a gap as possible between the pieces. Begin at one corner and continue all the way around.

3. Allow to set at least 24 hours.

4. If any adhesive shows through, paint it to match the frame.

Substitutions
Use a different frame size or shape.

How do I make a pique assiette piece?

What you need to get started:

Tesserae

China, floral pattern: cups (3), plates

Additional Supplies

Acrylic paints: fuchsia, white
Clean dry cloth
Grout, cement-based, sanded: white
Heavy welding compound
Multipurpose adhesive
Paintbrush
Picture hanger
Polymer clay: white
Precut wooden plaque with scalloped edges, 10" x 7"
PVA adhesive

In this technique you will use the "safety smash" to break the china. The pique assiette piece is grouted and follows the andamento "flow" of Opus Palladianum.

Wall Hook

Here's how:

1. Refer to Wood on page 19. Key and prep the wood.

2. Attach hanger to back of plaque, as it will be difficult to do so once the hooks are on.

3. Refer to Cutting China/Crockery on pages 29–30. Break plates and cups, breaking handles off the cup at the base and midway on the curve.

4. Mold a small amount of polymer clay over the broken tips of three cup handles. These will be the hooks.

5. Center and evenly space hooks on plaque. Attach hooks onto plaque with heavy welding compound.

6. Refer to Pique assiette on page 18. Attach the broken pieces onto plaque with multipurpose adhesive.

7. Allow to set at least 24 hours.

8. Mix fuchsia paint with white grout to desired color.

9. Refer to Grouting with Cement-based Sanded Grout on pages 31–32. Grout; allow to set.

Note: Remember to use a light touch to avoid scratching the china.

10. Paint the unfinished edges and back of the piece with fuchsia.

11. Mix a 1:1 wash with white paint and water. Brush over entire piece. Quickly wipe paint off surface of china pieces with a clean dry cloth.

Substitutions

Purchase a preassembled coat hanger and mosaic the base around the hooks.

Use different items for hangers (e.g. drawer pulls, china lids/handles, bent spoons, etc.).

41

How do I use andamento in my design?

What you need to get started:

Tesserae

China plate
Stained glass: blue mix
Tiles, tiny: black, white
Vitreous tiles: dark green, light
    green, medium green

Additional Supplies

Concrete stepping stone, 12"
    diameter
Grout, cement-based, sanded:
    gray to match stone
Grout sealer
Heavy-duty construction
    adhesive
Wheel glass cutter/nipper

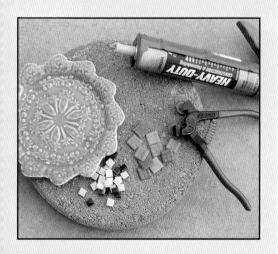

In this project, you will learn how to create a design by first completing your focal point (the flower) and then choosing a complementary andamento to fill in the background.

Stepping Stone

Here's how:

Note: A premade stepping stone was used for this project to avoid having to explain the steps necessary for the pour-your-own-mold types; if you are interested in the latter, you can find many excellent books on the subject.

1. Refer to Cutting China/Crockery on pages 29–30. Cut the plate, leaving the center intact.

2. Cut the plate rim into circles to form petals.

3. Attach the tiny tiles in an alternating pattern (black, white, black, etc.) around the edge of the stone to frame the design.

4. Attach the plate center onto the top third of the stone, then attach the petals around it.

5. Refer to Cutting Vitreous Tile on page 30. Cut vitreous tiles into rectangles. Arrange and attach the rectangles onto the stone to form the stem and grass.

6. Refer to Cutting Glass on page 28. Cut stained glass into random shapes.

7. Refer to Andamento/ Opus Palladianum on page 17. Loosely fill in the background with stained-glass shapes.

8. Allow to set at least 24 hours.

7

9. Refer to Grouting with Cement-based Sanded Grout on pages 31–32. Grout; allow to set.

10. Seal the grout and stone.

Substitutions

You can use stepping stones in different shapes (square, octagonal, etc.) and modify your design to fit the shape.

Create your own design that will fit on a stepping stone and use different types and colors of tesserae.

How do I mosaic a picture under glass?

What you need to get started:

Tesserae
Clear beveled glass, 16" square

Additional Supplies
Acrylic paints: dark green, light green, off-white
Acrylic crackle texture medium
Cherries print, 9" x 13"
Grout, cement-based, sanded: white
Masking tape
Miter saw
Paintbrushes
Picture hanger
Piece of wood, 9¹/₂" x 13¹/₂"
Silicone adhesive
Spray adhesive
Spray sealant
Tape measure
Trim molding
Wheel glass cutter/nipper
Wood glue

In this quick and easy mosaic technique you will attach clear glass tesserae directly onto the front of your chosen print, encasing the picture under the glass.

Country Cherries

Designed by Suzy Skadburg

Here's how:

1. Spray adhesive onto back side of print, covering the entire surface. Center and adhere print onto wood, making certain to eliminate all lumps or air bubbles. If necessary, use a ruler or the back of a spoon to smooth it out.

2. Refer to Cutting Glass on page 28. Cut beveled glass into approximately 1"-square tesserae.

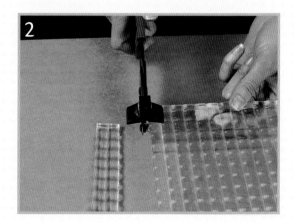

3. Apply a bead of silicone adhesive across the top of the print. Press the glass squares into the adhesive. Working in rows, continue attaching the glass from the top to the bottom.

Note: If your picture has a feature, like a face or an eye, make certain to maneuver the glass so you are placing the feature in the center of the square. If you do not, you will lose it in a grout line.

4. Allow to set at least 24 hours.

5. Measure trim molding to fit around mosaic. Cut molding to measurements with miter saw.

6. Apply a bead of wood glue along outside edge of mosaic. Press molding into glue to create picture frame. Allow to set 24 hours.

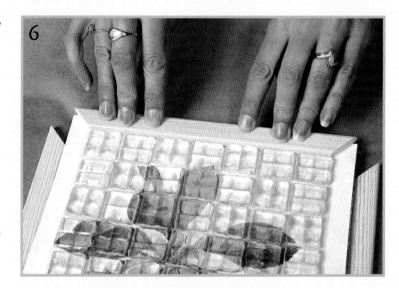

7. Refer to Grouting with Cement-based Sanded Grout on pages 31–32. Grout; allow to set.

8. Cover mosaic with masking tape to avoid getting paint on the glass or grout.

9. Paint trim with off-white. Allow to dry.

10. Paint trim with crackle texture medium. Allow to dry until tacky.

11. Mix dark green and light green paint to make an olive green color. Paint trim with olive green. The paint will begin to crackle so the off-white color shows through. Allow to dry.

Note: Make certain to only brush paint over an area once to avoid mixing it with the crackle texture medium.

12. Spray sealant over molding. Allow to dry and remove masking tape.

13. Attach a picture hanger onto back of mosaic.

Substitutions
Use a different print and paint colors for trim.

How do I mosaic in a picture frame?

A picture frame provides a perfect recess for holding a mosaic design. Simply adhere the plate glass into the frame to give yourself a base onto which you can attach the tesserae.

Framed Wild Heart (See photo on page 49)

Here's how:

1. Refer to Glass on page 19. Prep the glass surface.

2. Refer to Cutting Glass on page 28. Cut one piece of clear glass into approximately $3/8$"-square tesserae. Cut some of the squares into a few sharp triangular tesserae.

3. Attach tesserae onto patterned paper, leaving spaces between the pieces.

4. Allow to set at least 24 hours.

5. Cut stained glass into $5/8$"-square tesserae.

6. Apply a bead of adhesive along the recess on the inside of the frame. Adhere the remaining piece of clear glass inside the frame so grout will not seep out.

7. Allow to set at least 24 hours.

What you need to get started:

Tesserae
Plate glass: clear, 5" x 7" (2)
Stained glass: jade

Additional Supplies
Cork-backed metal ruler
Craft knife
Denatured alcohol
Glass cutter
Grout, cement-based, sanded: black
Marking pen
Masking tape
Patterned paper: leopard print
Picture frame with 5" x 7" picture opening
Silicone adhesive
Wheel glass cutter/nipper
Wooden skewer

8. Center and draw a heart design on front side of glass in frame, using the marking pen.

Note: If you do not like the way the drawing turned out, use denatured alcohol to remove the marks and start over.

9. Using a craft knife, cut the paper around each clear glass tessera until paper is flush with the glass.

10. Attach the papered tesserae onto the heart drawing, paper side down. Begin by outlining the heart, then fill in the center.

11. Refer to Andamento/Opus Tessellatum on page 17. Fill in the background with the stained glass. Trim some of the squares to fit around the heart shape.

Notes: Using a simple opus will give your piece good contrast.

If you are afraid your edges will not be uniform, you can cut a wooden skewer and lay it along the outside edge of the piece. Just remember to remove it before grouting.

12. Allow to set at least 24 hours.

13. Cover the picture frame with masking tape to keep it clean and undamaged during grouting.

14. Refer to Grouting with Cement-based Sanded Grout on pages 31–32. Grout; allow to set.

15. Remove masking tape.

Substitutions
You can substitute many simple designs for the one we used (e.g. a star, sun, crescent moon, etc.).

Be aware of how the frame you choose affects your design. Avoid choosing a frame that will take attention away from your piece. Think about where you will display your piece and how it will fit in that room.

Experiment with different patterned papers for endless design possibilities.

10–11

13

49

6
technique

What you need to get started:

Tesserae

Transparent millefiori, ³/₈"
  pieces
Transparent stained glass:
  dark blue, light blue, light
  green, lavender, teal

Additional Supplies

Cork-backed metal ruler
Glass cutter
Grout, cement-based, sanded:
  gray
Grout sealer
Light fixture with clear glass
  cover
Multipurpose adhesive
Wheel glass cutter/nipper

How do I mosaic glass on glass?

Attaching your glass tesserae onto a glass surface allows the light to shine through and show off their true beauty. Use a multipurpose adhesive and small tesserae when working on a glass surface.

Stained-glass Light Cover

Here's how:

1. Refer to Cutting Glass on page 28. Cut stained glass into approximately ⁵/₈"-square tesserae.

Note: Keep the colors separated in small containers for ease in working.

2. Refer to Glass on page 19. Prep the glass surface of the cover.

3. Attach the millefiori around the bottom edge of the cover.

4. Attach each color, one row at a time, using the following pattern from the millefiori row up to the top of the light cover: one row of lavender, one row of light blue, one row of light green, one row of all colors alternating, one row of teal, one row of lavender, one row of light blue, and one row of light green.

Note: Remember to leave the top edge uncovered so it will fit into the light fixture.

5. Allow to set at least 24 hours.

6. Refer to Grouting with Cement-based Sanded Grout on pages 31–32. Grout; allow to set.

7. Seal the grout.

Substitution
Use different colors and patterns of glass in your design.

How do I make a mosaic using pebbles?

What you need to get started:

Tesserae

Found object (we used a flamingo)
Pebbles: dark gray, white

Additional Supplies

Acrylic paint to match found
   object
Caulk/adhesive, exterior grade:
   gray or white
Marking pen
Picture hanger
Spray sealant: clear gloss
Wooden plaque, 7" x 24"

Pebbles give a project a natural, folksy feel. You can collect the small rocks yourself or you can purchase them in bags at hardware stores. For this project, they are self-grouted—pressed into caulk.

Pebble House Number

Here's how:

1. Refer to Wood on page 19. Key and prep the wood.

2. Attach hanger to back of wood.

3. Attach found object onto plaque where desired.

4. Draw house numbers on plaque, using the marking pen.

5. Apply a bead of caulk/adhesive over the numbers.

6. Press white stones into the caulk/adhesive to create the house numbers.

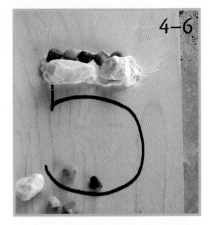

7. Apply adhesive and fill in around the found object with pebbles.

8. Apply adhesive onto the base, small sections at a time, and randomly place pebbles.

9. Allow to set at least 24 hours.

10. Seal as necessary with spray sealant to give the pebbles a shiny finish. Apply two or more coats.

11. Paint the edges of plaque to match the found object.

How do I mosaic with different uniform shapes?

What you need to get started:

Tesserae

Stained glass:
amber transparent, amethyst transparent, clear textured iridescent

Additional Supplies

Acrylic paint: purple
Clear glass cake stand with cover
Grout, cement-based, sanded: white
Grout additive
Marking pen
Multipurpose adhesive
Wheel glass cutter/nipper

A lovely border was created on the lower edge of this cake stand by rotating the tesserae of the first accent color 45° to form a diamond shape and by cutting the tesserae of the second accent color into triangles.

Cake Stand

Here's how:

1. Refer to Cutting Glass on page 28. Cut stained glass into approximately 1"- and ½"-square tesserae.

Note: Keep the colors separated in small containers for ease in working.

2. Refer to Glass on page 19. Prep the surfaces of the cake stand and cover.

3. Draw design on underside of glass, using the marking pen, if you feel you need the guidance.

4. Apply a bead of adhesive approximately ½" from the bottom edge of the cover all around.

5. Rotate large amethyst pieces so they look like diamonds and press them into the adhesive.

6. Cut large amber pieces into triangles and attach them in the upper and lower spaces between the amethyst diamonds.

7. Attach approximately four rows of large clear pieces, one row at a time, from the upper amber triangle row to the top of the side edge.

Note: The process of starting from the bottom and proceeding up helps to keep the design even. Also, it ensures that the higher tesserae do not slide down.

8. Attach approximately five rows of small clear pieces, one row at a time, from the top of the side edge to the handle on the cake stand.

9. Apply a bead of adhesive along the bottom edge of the stand's base. Press one row of small amber pieces into the adhesive. Attach remaining small pieces, one row at a time, from the bottom row to the top of the stand's base. Use the following pattern from the bottom up: three more rows of amber, one row of amethyst, one row of clear, and one row of amethyst.

10. Allow to set at least 24 hours.

11. Mix a very small amount of paint with white grout to tint the grout a light shade of lavender.

12. Refer to Grouting with Cement-based Sanded Grout on pages 31–32. Grout with additive and allow to set.

Substitution

If you think you need a little more working time, you can use silicone adhesive instead of multipurpose; it is just as good but does not dry as quickly. It will not cause sliding; you just have to make certain you get a strong attachment.

How do I mosaic a three-dimensional object?

Choose a base with fairly simple curves and dimensions as it facilitates the process of attaching the tesserae. Work the tesserae in rows first around the bottom, then around the top. Finally, fill in the space in the middle.

Dressmaker Form (See photo on page 58)

Here's how:

1. Refer to Bases on pages 18–20. Prep the form's surface.

2. Refer to Cutting Glass on page 28. Cut stained glass into approximately $\frac{1}{2}$"-square tesserae.

3. Apply a bead of adhesive around the bottom edge of the form.

4. Press the ribbon into the adhesive so the fringe hangs down freely and allow to set.

3–4

5. Attach one row of tesserae, with as little space as possible between pieces, over the ribbon of the bead fringe.

Note: This is the trick to using fringe; it helps ensure grout will not get into the beads.

What you need to get started:

Tesserae
Leaf beads
Marbles
Rhinestone
Stained glass: black iridescent, red iridescent, white iridescent

Additional Supplies
Acrylic paint: plum
Beaded fringe
Cork-backed metal ruler
Dressmaker form, small
Glass cutter
Grout, cement-based, sanded: black
Grout additive
Paintbrushes
Silicone adhesive
Wheel glass cutter/nipper

6. Attach the tesserae, one row at a time, as desired onto the form. Begin from the bottom and work up a few rows. Move to the top and work down a few rows. Then fill in the middle.

Note: This will help ensure an even look to the finished piece by regulating your flow.

7. Allow to set at least 24 hours.

8. Refer to Grouting with Cement-based Sanded Grout on pages 31–32. Grout with additive and allow to set.

Note: Take care to avoid getting grout on the fringe.

9. Paint the pole and stand plum.

Substitutions
Use a different-shaped form for your base. Be careful to select one that does not have too many different curves or angles as this can make it difficult to achieve an even surface with the tesserae.

Experiment with various types of trims, placing them along the edges of your form.

Here are a few examples of three-dimensional objects that can be mosaicked. **Left:** A pot that has flat or squared-off sides makes it easier to achieve a flat mosaic surface. Use the double-reverse method on pages 82–85 to keep motifs on painted tiles intact.

Bottom left: The delicate blue floral pattern on the tiles selected to cover this vase softens the appearance of the irregular surface. The pattern, which was achieved using the double-reverse method, repeats itself in the round and is accented by a row of blue tiles at the bottom of the vase.

Bottom right: These rounded lanterns are covered with various colors of stained-glass tesserae. Because the lanterns each have a glass base on which the tesserae is attached (similar to the Stained-glass Light Cover on pages 50–51), the light will shine through them when they are lit up at night—the perfect accessories for your next outdoor party.

Section 3: beyond the basics

How do I combine found objects with pique assiette?

What you need to get started:

Tesserae
Ceramic roses
China, floral pattern
Tile

Additional Supplies
Acrylic paints: pale pink, white
Grout, cement-based, sanded:
  white
Masking tape, 1"-wide
Mastic, thin-set, interior grade
Paintbrushes
Tile nippers
Wheel glass cutter/nipper
Wooden serving tray

The pique-assiette style of mosaic makes it easy to add an object of almost any size or shape into the design. Simply trim the abutting tesserae to fit around the object and continue on.

Tile & Roses Tray

Designed by Suzy Skadburg

Here's how:

1. Refer to Wood on page 19. Key and prep the wood.

2. Paint tray white, excluding inside bottom panel, which will be covered with mosaic, and allow to dry.

3. Refer to Cutting China/Crockery on pages 29–30. Break plates.

4. Refer to Cutting Tile on page 29. Cut tile into random shapes.

5. Refer to Pique assiette on page 18. Attach the tesserae onto inside bottom panel with

mastic, beginning in one corner with a tile piece that has two straight sides to match the corner and building on from that point until panel is covered.

Note: Randomly place ceramic roses throughout the design.

6. Allow to set at least 24 hours.

7. Refer to Grouting with Cement-based Sanded Grout on pages 31–32 Grout; allow to set.

Note: Remember to use a light touch to avoid scratching the china or breaking the roses.

8. To create stripes around sides of tray, begin at corner of one outside edge and apply three strips of masking tape vertically, one next to the other. Remove the center strip of tape. Continue in this manner around the tray.

9. Paint exposed "stripes" pale pink and allow to dry. Remove tape.

10. Attach several ceramic roses as desired onto inside edge of tray handles and allow to set.

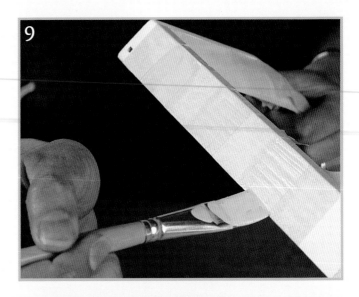

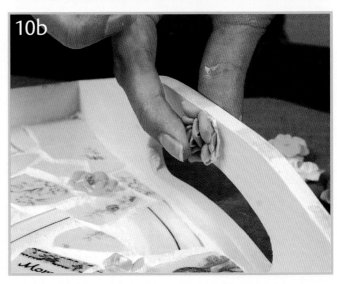

How do I combine found objects with a mirror?

When you are using a mirror in your mosaic, choose a few specific tesserae to complement and balance the shine of the mirror so it does not overwhelm the other elements in the piece. Shiny filigree buttons do the trick for this project.

Jeweled Mirror (See photo on page 67)

Here's how:

1. Using the geometry set, establish the center on the wood base, then mark off an "X."

2. Draw a 6" circle in the center for mirror placement.

Note: You can use a slightly larger mirror to help with the placement of the first ring of beads.

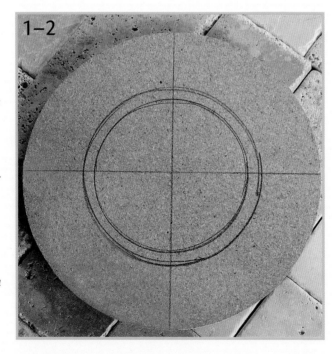

1–2

3. Refer to Wood on page 19. Key and prep the wood.

4. Attach hanger onto back of wooden circle.

What you need to get started:

Tesserae

Filigree beads: gold
Filigree buttons: gold (4)
Marbles: white
Stained glass: pink iridescent, white iridescent

Additional Supplies

Acrylic paints: black, white
Clean dry cloth
Cork-backed metal ruler
Geometry set
Glass cutter
Grout, cement-based, sanded: black
Mirror, 6" diameter
Picture hanger
Spray sealant: clear gloss
Wheel glass cutter/nipper
Wooden circle, 12" diameter

5. Refer to Cutting Glass on page 28. Cut stained glass.

6. Seal filigree beads and buttons with spray sealant.

Note: You can do this before or after you attach them—just remember to seal them before you attach any glass or marbles as the sealant will leave a film on the glass tesserae.

7. Attach filigree buttons at 3, 6, 9, and 12 o'clock onto the wooden circle.

8. Working in rings, attach the tesserae with the first ring around the mirror placement, the second ring around the outside edge, then fill in the middle.

Note: When setting the buttons and beads, remember to use more adhesive to ensure a strong attachment and avoid the possibility of losing them when grouting.

9. Attach mirror onto center.

10. Allow to set at least 24 hours.

11. Refer to Grouting with Cement-based Sanded Grout on pages 31–32. Grout; allow to set.

12. Mix a 1:1 wash with white paint and water. Brush over entire piece except the mirror. Quickly wipe paint off surface of glass pieces with a clean dry cloth.

13. Paint back of piece with black.

Substitutions
Use a different shape for your mirror such as a square, rectangle, or oval.

Select tesserae to match the decor of the room in which you will place the mirror.

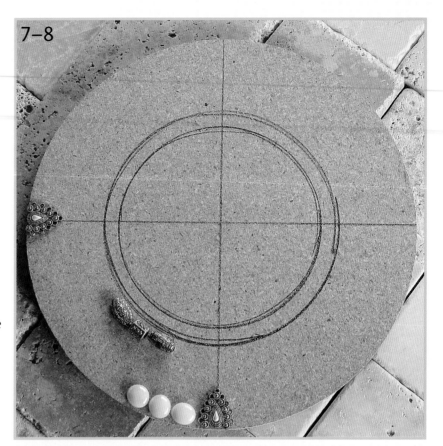

7–8

8–9

3
project

How do I mix andamento opuses?

What you need to get started:

Tesserae

Found objects: ceramic rose, small flamingo, etc.
Marbles: clear
Millefiori: multicolored
Stained glass: teal
Tiny tiles: blue, green
Vitreous tiles: blue, green, white

Additional Supplies

Acrylic paint: yellow
Cork-backed metal ruler
Glass cutter
Grout, cement-based, sanded: white
Patterned paper
Silicone adhesive
Wheel glass cutter/nipper
Wooden birdhouse: small

This birdhouse, which has several different sides, naturally lends itself to varied applications of andamenti. The combination of distinct and separate patterns results in a visually stimulating piece.

Love Nest

Here's how:

1. Refer to Wood on page 19. Key and prep the wood.

2. Refer to Cutting Glass on page 28. Cut stained glass into randomly sized pieces.

3. Attach ceramic rose above the hole onto the birdhouse.

4. Attach millefiori around the hole.

5. Attach other found objects as desired.

6. Refer to "How do I mosaic in a picture frame?" Steps 3–4, and 9 on pages 47–48. Attach paper to marbles, then attach marbles around bottom of base.

7. Fill in front and back with tiny tiles.

8. Attach vitreous tiles onto roof for shingled look.

3–8

9. Attach randomly cut stained glass onto sides.

10. Allow to set at least 24 hours.

11. Mix yellow paint with white grout to desired color.

12. Refer to Grouting with Cement-based Sanded Grout on pages 31–32. Grout; allow to set.

Substitutions
Vary the design and lay out of your tesserae. Use a completely different color scheme.

Millefiori can be your starting point. There are many different patterns available. When you find one you like, choose the rest of your tesserae around that pattern.

How do I use mesh to make a mosaic?

What you need to get started:

Tesserae

Mirror: dark blue, light blue, medium blue, bronze, light bronze, light gold, orange, red, yellow

Additional Supplies

Cork-backed metal ruler
Glass cutter
Grout, cement-based, sanded: to match wall
Grout additive
Grout sealer
Masking tape
Marking pen, permanent
Mesh
Pencil
Plastic wrap (or other plastic sheeting)
Silicone adhesive
Wheel glass cutter/nipper

Mesh is essential when you are creating a mosaic that needs to be moved from one place to another. While in your own work space, you can attach tesserae onto the mesh. Once the design is complete, the entire piece can be moved to the final site.

Garden Sun

Here's how:

Note: Use this technique when you need to mosaic evenly onto an uneven or slightly curved surface. It also allows you to create the mosaic in your workshop and move it to its final location. Usually, it is also recommended that you pre-grout the piece before attaching it; however, if the final destination is not totally flat, this could cause a problem.

1. Enlarge and photocopy Garden Sun Pattern on page 73 to desired size.

2. Tape the drawing to the work surface.

3. Tape a piece of clear plastic over the drawing to protect it from adhesive.

4. Lay the mesh over the plastic; tape in place.

5. Draw the design onto the mesh, using the marking pen.

6. Cut mirror pieces into approximately 1"-square tesserae.

Note: Keep the colors separated in small containers for ease in working.

7. Refer to Andamento/Opus Musivum on page 17. Using silicone, attach the tesserae onto mesh. Alternate shades of blue for crescent; red and orange for sun; and shades of bronze, gold, and yellow for rays.

8. Allow to set for 2–3 hours, then flip over and remove the clear plastic so it does not stick permanently to the piece.

9. Allow to set for at least 24 hours.

10. Trim mesh to ¼" around the mosaic.

11. Refer to Bases on pages 18–20. Prep the surface.

Note: If the surface is flat, pregrout your piece before attaching it.

12. Hold the mosaic up to the surface and draw a light outline, using the pencil on the final location.

13. Mix epoxy resin, following the manufacturer's directions.

Note: Use a quick-set (5-minute) epoxy for vertical applications.

14. Spread a thin layer of epoxy inside the outline.

Note: Be aware that it will run a little if the area is not horizontal.

15. Quickly attach the piece onto the resin. Hold in place as necessary.

16. Allow resin to set completely (usually a couple of hours).

17. Refer to Grouting with Cement-based Sanded Grout on pages 31–32. Grout with additive and allow to set.

18. Seal the grout.

Substitution
You can mosaic this pattern using the direct method if you have access to the surface during the entire process.

Garden Sun Pattern

5
project

How do I make a mosaic using large and small tiles?

What you need to get started:

Tesserae

Tiles: tumbled travertine
3"-square tiles: speckled brown
  (2 shades), forest green,
  seafoam green, light purple,
  white, yellow

Additional Supplies

Grout, cement-based, sanded:
  pewter
Marking pen, permanent
Mastic, thin-set, exterior grade
Metal frame
Screwdriver
Tile nippers
Wood screws
Wooden panel

Since tiles are available in several different sizes and colors, you have almost unlimited options for mixing and matching to create a pleasing design. In this project, the large tiles frame the central daisies motif. The smaller, irregularly shaped tiles fill in the background in a "crazy paving" style.

Daisies Tile Picture

Designed by James Turner

Here's how:

1. Attach the wooden panel onto the metal frame, screwing onto the frame through the back.

2. Refer to Wood on page 19. Key and prep the wood.

3. Enlarge and photocopy Daisies Tile Picture Pattern on page 76 to the desired size. Use photocopy as a pattern to center and draw the design on the wood, using the permanent marker.

4. Refer to Cutting Tile on page 29. Cut and shape tiles.

5. According to the design, attach tiles onto wooden panel,

74

pressing firmly to ensure a good grip. Adhere the central motif and border first, then fill in the background, using random rectangles and squares.

Note: The look is casual—simply give it a random feel. Also, the artist has used a graduating color effect from the bottom right-hand corner to the top left-hand corner.

6. Allow to set at least 24 hours.

7. Refer to Grouting with Cement-based Sanded Grout on pages 31–32. Grout; allow to set.

Substitutions
Use the design of your choice in the same metal frame.

Change the look of the mosaic by choosing a different type frame.

Daisies Tile Picture Pattern

How do I use the indirect/reverse method?

The indirect/reverse method is used when you need to make certain the surface of the mosaic is perfectly flat. By first attaching the front side of the tesserae onto a piece of brown paper, then flipping the entire design over onto the adhesive, you can ensure that it will turn out to be level.

Wall Clock (See photo on page 81)

Here's how:

1. Center and drill a hole in the wooden panel.

2. Refer to Wood on page 19. Key and prep the wood.

3. Attach picture hanger onto back of wooden panel.

4. Enlarge and photocopy Wall Clock Pattern on page 80. Use photocopy as a pattern to reverse and draw the design on the brown paper.

5. Refer to Cutting Vitreous Tile on page 30. Cut tesserae from tiles.

6. According to the design, attach tesserae, face side down, onto brown paper with the diluted PVA.

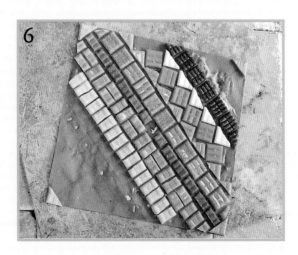

What you need to get started:

Tesserae
Vitreous tiles: shades of blue, shades of green, white, yellow

Additional Supplies
Acrylic paints: royal blue, silver
Brown paper
Clockwork
Grout, cement-based, sanded: bone
Mallet
Miniature metal fork and spoon
Notched spreader
Picture hanger
Power drill
PVA adhesive diluted 1:1 with water
Silicone adhesive
Sponge
Wheel glass cutter/nipper
Wooden board, small
Wooden panel, 8" square

7. Allow to set 2–3 hours.

8. Using a notched spreader, evenly apply adhesive onto the base.

9. Place the mosaic, with paper side up, on the base.

10. Place the wooden board over the mosaic and tap it with the mallet to make the piece even.

11. Allow to set at least 24 hours.

12. Wet and ring out a sponge, then dampen the paper.

Note: Do not soak the paper. You are only trying to break down the adhesive's grip.

13. Gently peel the paper off; if it does not come off easily, dampen it a bit more.

14. Gently wipe the glue residue from the mosaic.

15. Mix blue paint with bone grout to desired color.

16. Refer to Grouting with Cement-based Sanded Grout on pages 31–32. Grout; allow to set.

17. Clear the grout out of the central hole when it is dry.

18. After cleaning, attach the clockwork.

Note: It is a good idea to run a little clear adhesive over the grout in the center hole to keep small particles from getting into the works.

19. Paint clock hands silver.

20. Attach miniature fork and spoon onto clock hands.

21. Paint the back or the piece with blue.

Substitutions
Use a multipurpose adhesive.

Use the direct method for this project.

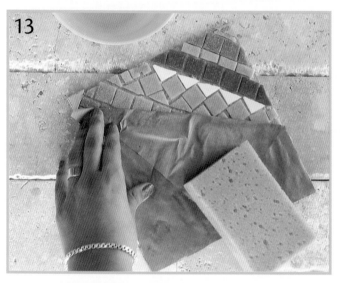

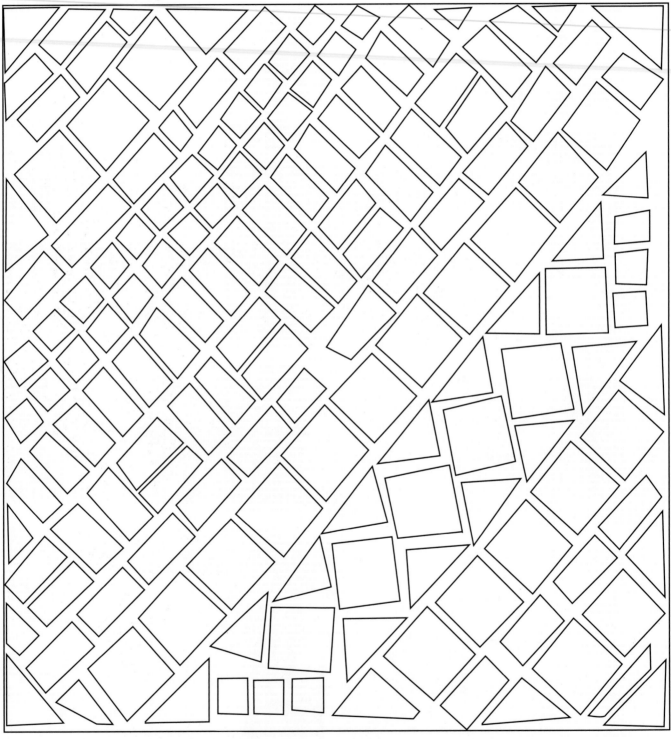

project

How do I use the double-reverse method?

What you need to get started:

Tesserae
China plate, square

Additional Supplies
Acrylic paints: off-white, orange
Contact paper
Grout, cement-based, sanded: white
Grout additive
Grout sealer
Mallet
Metal plant stand, square, small
Multipurpose adhesive
Notched spreader
Wooden board, small
Wooden piece to fit into plant stand frame

Breath new life into an overlooked piece of furniture like this plant stand by removing its "ho-hum" top and replacing it with mosaic made from a broken china plate. This technique shows you how easy it can be to keep the plate's pattern intact and transfer it onto your furniture piece.

Greenhouse Side Table

Here's how:

1. Remove the existing top from the plant stand.

2. Place wooden piece into frame and attach with multipurpose adhesive for the mosaic base.

3. Seal around the edges with multi-purpose adhesive to keep the grout from seeping.

4. Cut two pieces from contact paper slightly larger than the mosaic base.

2–3

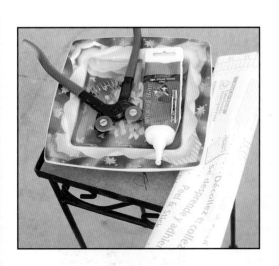

5. Refer to Cutting China/Crockery on pages 29–30. Break plate and reassemble, picture side up, on one piece of contact paper.

6. Lay remaining piece of contact paper over the assembled pieces; make certain they are attached well.

7. Flip over and carefully remove the contact paper from the back side.

8. Apply adhesive very thickly onto the base in the frame, using a notched spreader to even it out. Make certain to apply it thick enough to be able to set all the china pieces into it and maintain a flat surface.

9. Flip mosaic over and place pieces into adhesive, picture side up.

10. Place the wooden board over the mosaic and tap it with the mallet to make the piece even.

11. Allow to set at least 24 hours.

Note: The piece may need at least two days to set because of the thickness of the adhesive.

12. Remove the contact paper.

13. Mix orange paint with bone grout to desired color.

14. Refer to Grouting with Cement-based Sanded Grout on pages 31–32. Grout with additive; allow to set.

15. Seal grout.

16. Paint the plant stand with off-white and orange paint as desired.

Substitutions

Keep an eye out at bed-and-bath stores and garden stores for metal plant stands; they frequently sell small ones for under $20.

If you want to use a round metal table that does not have a frame, you can purchase a round metal hoop from a craft store in the correct diameter to "frame" the table. (See Photo A on page 85) Attach the hoop onto the table with heavy-duty adhesive and you are ready to go.

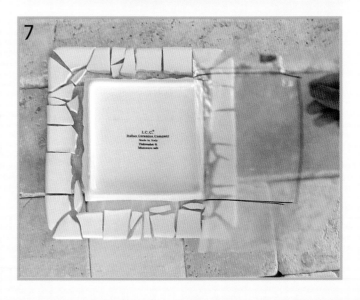

85

8 project

What you need to get started:

Tesserae
Stained glass: various colors, same thicknesses

Additional Supplies
Bonding mortar, interior/exterior grade: gray
Grout, cement-based, sanded: gray
Grout float, rubber
Notched trowel
Plastic containers
Stir sticks
Wheel glass cutter/nipper

How do I use bonding mortar on an exterior surface?

Because this project will be subjected to foot traffic, you need to use an adhesive with a very strong and lasting grip. Bonding mortar is such an adhesive. It was used here to attach various sized and colored stained-glass tesserae in the area between a sidewalk and the front door of a boutique.

Stained-glass Threshold

Designed by Areta Bingham

Here's how:

Note: This threshold used to be tiled. The tile was removed and the mosaic was placed in the existing recess. If you would like to create a similar threshold, you may need to consult a contractor as how to create a recess so the completed mosaic is flush and level with your floor(s). However, if you would like to do this technique on a step or enclosed patio, simply place it on top of the existing surface, thereby building up the surface.

1. Thoroughly clean area where you will be applying the mosaic design. Make certain all dust and debris are removed.

2. Refer to Cutting Glass on page 28. Cut all glass into uniformly sized tesserae, using the wheel glass cutter/nipper.

Notes: Keep the colors separated in small containers for ease in working.

While you are placing the glass in the design, you may find you need a special shape or size. Simply custom-cut the desired piece with the wheel glass cutter/nipper.

3. Pour a small amount of bonding mortar into a plastic container, add a little cool water, and mix with a stir stick. Continue adding water until your mortar is the consistency of a smooth paste. Let stand 5–10 minutes, and stir again.

Note: Stir occasionally to keep fluffy but do not add more water. When mixed properly, troweled edges will stand with little or no slump.

4. Working a small area at a time, apply mortar onto surface with flat side of trowel held at a 40˚ angle to force mortar into irregularities in the surface. Slide the notched side of the trowel over the mortar. Press tesserae into mortar, allow to dry. Repeat process until the entire surface is covered.

Note: Do not spread more mortar than you can apply glass onto in 15 minutes.

5. Allow to set for at least 24 hours.

6. Refer to Grouting with Cement-based Sanded Grout on pages 31–32. Holding a rubber grout float at a 45° angle, grout until all spaces are completely filled. Remove excess grout, using the edge of the float at a 90° angle.

Substitution

Use large stencils as patterns for cutting numbers and floral motifs from stained glass. As you construct your threshold, press the numbers and motifs into the mortar or cement to create a unique street address.

How do I create my own colored glass?

Can't find the exact color of glass to match your home decor? Make it yourself with clear plate glass and a bit of acrylic paint.

Painted-glass Side Table (See photo on page 91)

Designed by Suzy Skadburg

Here's how:

1. Measure trim moulding to fit around tabletop. Cut molding to measurements with miter saw.

2. Apply a bead of wood glue along outside edge of tabletop. Press molding into glue to create a recessed top. Allow to set 24 hours.

3. Using paintbrush and paints, paint front, sides, and legs of table as shown in the photo on page 91 or as desired.

4. Refer to Wood on page 19. Key and prep the table top.

5. Paint one side of plate glass bright green, reserving two 4" squares, painting one lavender and the other purple.

What you need to get started:

Tesserae

Plate glass, clear, 24" square

Additional Supplies

Acrylic paints: black, bright green, lavender, magenta, orange, purple, white
Grout, cement-based, sanded: white
Mallet
Miter saw
Mastic, thin-set, interior grade
Notched spreader
Paintbrush
Tape measure
Trim molding, 1/2" wider than tabletop
Wheel glass cutter/nipper
Wood glue
Wooden board, small
Wooden side table

6. Refer to Cutting Glass on page 28. Cut all glass into uniformly sized tesserae, using the wheel glass cutter/nipper.

Notes: Keep the colors separated in small containers for ease in working.

While you are positioning the tesserae in the design, you may find you need a special shape or size. Simply custom-cut the desired piece with the wheel glass cutter/nipper.

7. Apply mastic onto painted side of the lavender- and the purple-colored tesserae. Arrange the pieces to form a rose at the center of the table front. Apply mastic onto the painted side of three or four pieces of bright-green-colored tesserae and place them at the outside edge of the rose for leaves.

Note: This table has a knob on the front panel which was perfect for building the rose around.

8. Beginning at one corner, working a small area at a time, and using a notched spreader, evenly apply mastic onto the tabletop. Press bright-green-colored tesserae, painted side down, into the mastic. Place the wooden board over the mosaic and tap it with the mallet to ensure that the tesserae are even. Repeat process until the entire surface is covered.

Note: Do not spread more mastic than you can apply glass onto in 15 minutes.

9. Allow to set for at least 24 hours.

10. Refer to Grouting with Cement-based Sanded Grout on pages 31–32. Grout; allow to set.

Substitutions
Use glass paint to create different effects in the colored-glass tesserae.

Paint a complete picture in reverse on the glass, then use the double/reverse method on pages 82–85 to apply the mosaic onto your chosen surface.

6

7

8–10

How do I mosaic on a vertical surface?

What you need to get started:

Tesserae

Found objects: beads, buttons, jewels, etc.
Ceramic bowls, cups, and plates
Marbles: assorted colors
Terra-cotta pots
Tiles: assorted colors and sizes

Additional Supplies

Acrylic paint: off-white
Ceramic tile adhesive
Notched trowel
Plastic containers
Sponge
Stir sticks
Mastic, thin-set, exterior grade: white
Wheel glass cutter/nipper

This project is a wonderful example of how you can use the direct method to create a mosaic on a wall. Simply attach an assortment of tesserae onto the surface with tile adhesive, then fill in the spaces with thin-set mastic. This lively backsplash was created in one afternoon.

Hodgepodge Backsplash

Designed by Suzy Skadburg

Here's how:

1. Refer to Cutting tesserae on pages 28–30. Cut or break tiles and found objects as desired.

2. Randomly attach larger pieces of tesserae, such as half bowls and cups, onto wall with tile adhesive.

Note: If necessary, use masking tape to help secure the larger tesserae pieces while the adhesive dries.

3. Allow to set at least 24 hours.

4. Pour a small amount of mastic into a plastic container, add a little cool water, and mix with a stir stick. Continue adding water until mastic is the consistency of peanut butter. Let stand 5–10 minutes, and stir again.

Note: Stir occasionally to keep fluffy but do not add more water. When mixed properly, tesserae will stand in mastic with little or no slump.

5. Mix off-white paint with mastic to desired color.

6. Working a small area at a time, apply mastic onto the wall, approximately $1/4$"–$1/2$" thick, using notched trowel. Randomly position tesserae into mastic; allow to dry. Repeat process until the entire surface is covered.

Note: Do not spread more mastic than you can apply tesserae onto in 15 minutes.

7. Wet a sponge, then wipe excess mastic off tesserae.

8. Allow to set at least 24 hours.

Substitution
Try this technique with a planned layout such as an expanded geometric design like the Wall Clock on pages 77–81 or the Daisies Tile Picture on pages 74–76.

 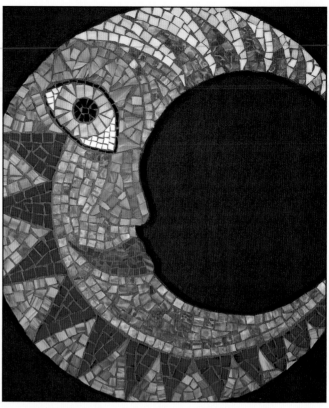

Section 4: the gallery

95

married to a real cowboy for many years and spent long hours observing rodeos, team penning, and team roping events. How natural then to make artwork of cowboys and cowgirls, boots, bulls, and spurs. Although this is not the only theme of her mosaics, it is certainly the dominant theme so far.

Sheila loves every part of the mosaicking process, from shopping for ceramic that can be broken and made into a wonderful palette of colors, to designing the piece, to the tedious yet satisfying job of shaping and setting the tesserae, to grouting the mosaic. She credits the success of her mosaic work to the solid principles of design, composition, value, and color that she has learned from creating award-winning works with other mediums and a strong commitment to good craftsmanship. A great work of art, be it a painting or a mosaic, will always have a good composition, wonderful color and values, and interesting shapes and patterns. Because making mosaics is relatively new to Sheila, she is looking forward to exploring the endless potential of this medium.

Sheila Hudson began her career as an artist working primarily in pure transparent watercolor. Finally, after feeling the need for more layers of interest in her work, she added other mediums such as colored pencil, acrylic, ink, paper collage, etc. Combining a well-developed personal style and hard work, she has entered many juried shows and won many awards over the years with both watercolor and mixed-media paintings.

Somewhere along the way she became interested in making mosaics. Interestingly, although she does most of her mosaic work in the same whimsical style as many of her paintings, she has incorporated a western theme in her mosaics that had never shown up in her work before. It is actually surprising that the western theme did not show up earlier since Sheila has been

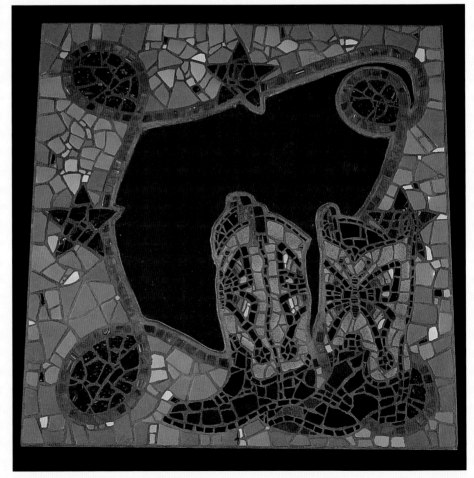

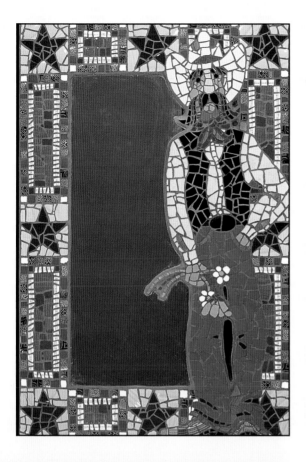 

 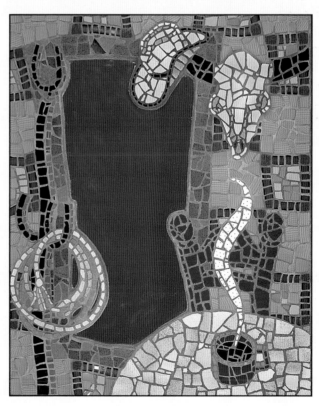

James Turner started mosaicking in 1996 to keep himself busy when he was not rowing a drift boat as a professional fly-fishing guide. A Montana native, he now runs a mosaic studio and a shop selling handcrafted furniture in Boise, Idaho.

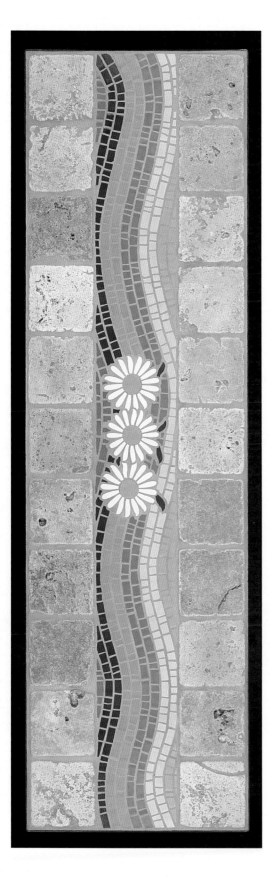

Miriam Woito describes her work as an attempt to reflect the beauty of the world around her. She recently returned from living in England for four years and spending time traveling extensively. She was inspired by the different peoples and their cultures—the way they expressed themselves visually through art work and architecture. She was impressed by the care and attention that was given to the aesthetics of the surroundings as there seemed to be an air of lasting elegance.

Through painting and collage work, Miriam tries strives to achieve several goals: to trigger memories; to bring together treasures; to create orderly chaos that can be explored; to reach into history an incorporate symbols and images that represent the important aspects of different ages; to combine these images to span the ages; to combine materials that play off one another; and to be thematic while exploring, in detail, different ideas, perspectives, and images.

In addition to collage work, Miriam enjoys painting portraits. In them, she attempts to capture the personality and image of the individual. She owns and operates and art school in Boise, Idaho, where she teaches both children and adults.

Miriam believes art to be a form of expression in which everyone can become articulate. For some it is the only means of self-expression. By doing and teaching art, she hopes to promote the importance of art in our society today.

Zella Bardsley's work in recycled steel is ecofeminist in theme, joyful, and celebratory. "My intent," she says, "is to convey that life is meant to be an adventure, filled with the various emotions we are gifted with."

Each work of art is born out of one or more slabs of recycled steel. Sometimes Zella applies paint (gleaned from a local construction company's mechanic shop) onto the steel to yield a particular visual effect. Then she cuts it with an oxygen and acetylene torch that leaves a sort of halo effect, grinds it, and assembles it with a MIG welder. She finishes most of her pieces with a polyurethane coating to prevent any rust.

Much of Zella's work is currently on display at select galleries in and around the city of Boise, Idaho, where she lives.

Zella holds a Master's Degree in Education from Boise State University, and has seven years teaching experience with the Department of Health and Welfare.

About the Author

Reham Aarti Jacobsen was born and raised in Kuwait and was fortunate enough to have a wonderfully artistic family. For Reham, her uncle, Mussa Aarti, was the most influential person of all because he is a master of mixed media, as she hopes to one day be. She now lives in Boise, Idaho, with her husband, Soren, son, Shahien, and stepson, Preston.

Reham's mosaicking career officially started in 1998 when her husband unexpectedly whisked her off to Berkeley, California, to take a private lesson from the renowned mosaic artist, Dmitry Grudsky, of the former Soviet Union. Since that time, she has spent countless hours developing techniques in her current passion—mosaics. She uses several kinds of tesserae in her work: stained glass, ceramic tile, beads, mirror, china, glass pebble—anything she can adhere and grout to a stable surface. Her work can now be seen in art galleries, gift shops, and on-line.

Because of her global upbringing, Reham tries to bring aspects of other cultures into her work. She loves to make large, colorful, stand-out pieces that seem to go over very well with the children in her life (including her husband). She likes to take an active role in her community, donating art to fund-raisers, and doing art projects with some of the area schools.

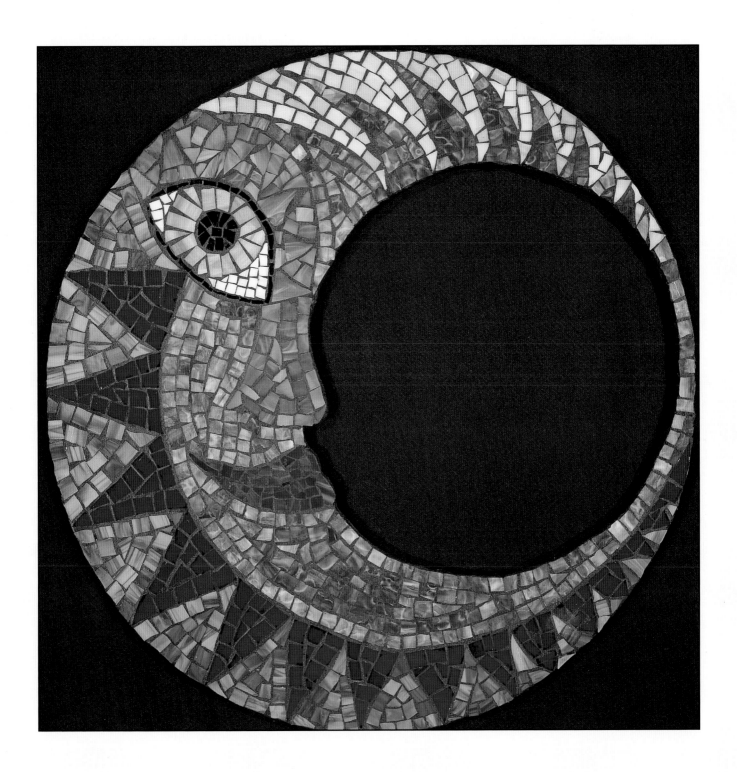

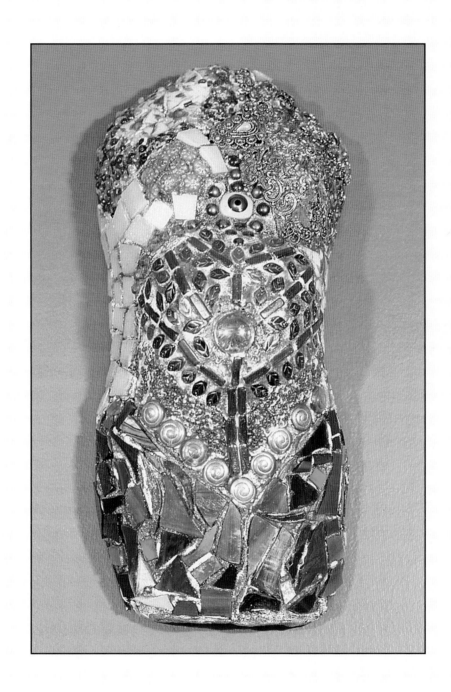

and to Caryn Rutherford for offering my art a home, helping with the "consumer" view, and for being an all-out awesome lady. You two are too amazing for words.

A huge thank-you to Becky Edwards without whom this book would not have come into my life—you are a fantastic artist as well. And thank-you to Chapelle, Ltd., for giving me this opportunity—it was a dream come true.

Thanks to Dustin, you have no idea how much I appreciate your help; and to James Turner, the best thing I ever got at any market, bar none. You are so solid in too many ways to count.

To my parents, Pat and Abbas Aarti, thank you for who I am, and for the fabulous genes that allow me to be an artist, as well as all the love and support you have lavished on me all these years. You gave me the confidence to do things like this. I love you both.

Author's Thanks

First and foremost, thank-you to my wonderful husband, Soren, for your help with everything to do with this book, for getting me started in mosaics, and for just being the you that I love. To my sons, Preston and Shahien, thank you for putting up with less "mom" time, and being so understanding when the outings lessened to a drizzle. I love you like crazy!

Special thanks to Melanie for meticulous grammar/punctuation help, and more importantly for being there for my boys; to my sister, Batul, and best friend, Heather, for sanity checks and kid time (and snacks/sushi). You three are off the hook.

Thank-you to P. J., Meagan, and Ashley for being the best kid brigade baby-sitting crew ever. Thank-you to Cindy Haroian for floors, time off, and being in my life in general;

Thank-you to Ron and Sharron (mom) Laursen, for being in my life and loving me, and for all the supplies. Thank-you to Zella Bardsley, who gave me courage in the beginning.

To all the family and friends who show their love and support every day in so many little ways: Cathy, Hank, and Jaryd; Pat, Ginger, and the entire Connoly crew; Cody, Scot, and Bracey; the Ocamicas (plus Missy); all my family back home and in the U.S.; Patrick J. Sandru; Linda, Dan, and Kelli Kerpa; Hossah, Khalid, and Tahani; and Woody and Robin Al-Haddad.

To the fuel-stop girls; to the lovely lady at Savers; to all of the artists who contributed to the gallery of this book; and to every person who picks up this book and accomplishes something beautiful—thank you with all my heart!

Glossary of Terms

Acrylic Paint: Water-based paint, used to paint bases and color cement-based grout.

Andamento: The "flow" or pattern in which tesserae are placed that makes up a mosaic picture.

Backerboard: Cement- or fiberglass-based panels used as a base for mosaic work when a water-resistant underlayment is necessary.

Buff: The practice of removing the haze or residue left on glass after initial removal of excess grout.

Butter: The practice of applying adhesive to each tessera before placing it, or spreading adhesive on a small area of the base.

Cure: The setting process of cement, grout, mortar, and adhesive; a chemical change that makes these substances gain strength.

Filati: Rods of glass made in Italy, manufactured for and used specifically in miniature mosaics.

Float: Tool used to spread grout or smooth out cement.

Grout: A mixture of sand, cement, and water used to fill spaces between tesserae; available in powdered or pre-mixed form.

Gum Arabic/Gum Mucilage: Water-based adhesive used to attach tesserae to paper for the reverse, or indirect, mosaic method.

Hammer and Hardi: A hammer and a type of anvil traditionally used to cut smalti and stone.

Key: Causing the roughness of a surface. To key a surface, one roughens it to provide a better grip between adhesive and tesserae.

Mastic: A premixed tile adhesive with a latex or petrochemical base.

MDF: Medium-density fiberboard.

Millefiori: Small round glass pieces with designs in the "face," cut from glass rods (similar to a polymer clay cane).

Micro Mosaic: A miniature mosaic traditionally made with smalti filati, but can also refer to a mosaic made with beads or other small pieces.

Mortar: A mixture of sand and cement.

Nibbling: The act of cutting, or nipping, small pieces away from the edges of tesserae to achieve a usually curved shape.

Opus Circumactum: Fan-shaped design; can be used to cover large expanses without the need for a "picture."

Opus Musivum: Essentially opus vermiculatum continued for the entire background; this gives a very lively look.

Opus Palladianum: Irregular tesserae laid out in the "crazy paving" tradition. The trick is to keep the spaces relatively equal between the tesserae. A great way to use up bits and pieces, but try not to overdue it or it loses its charm.

Opus Regulatum: To layout the tesserae in a grid; very plain yet dramatic when used properly.

Opus Sectile: More common among stained-glass artists, this opus uses pieces cut individually into shapes specifically fitted to each other.

Opus Spicatum: A weave or herringbone effect.

Opus Tessellatum: Where rows of the tesserae are laid in a staggered way, similar to brickwork. It is essential that the pieces do not match up or the effect is ruined.

Opus Vermiculatum: To outline your focal point or design and then the rest of the background; can be completed using opus regulatum or opus tessellatum.

Pique Assiette: A style of mosaic in which the base is covered with various sized and colored tesserae placed in a random pattern.

Pizze: Round or oval slabs of molten glass from which smalti is cut.

Plywood: A relatively inexpensive material made of thin layers of wood glued together.

PVA (polyvinyl acetate): Water-soluble craft glue used most often in the indirect, or reverse, mosaic method. When diluted 5:1 with water it can be used as a base sealant—especially for wood surfaces.

Sealant: A protective coating.

Slaking: Allowing the grout mixture to interact for at least 15 minutes before use in order to give the polymers time to strengthen and bind.

Smalti: Italian-made traditional mosaic tesserae made from molten glass.

Spatula: A wooden or plastic spreading tool; can also be used to mix grout.

Stiff Grout: The less water you add to grout the drier, or "stiffer," it is.

Tessera (*plural:* Tesserae): Originally used to describe a square or cupped piece of stone; now refers to all "pieces" used to make a mosaic. Tesserae are the basis of a mosaic.

Vitreous Tile: A mass-produced glass tile that is less expensive than smalti for use in mosaics. It is strong and durable, but not as vividly colored as smalti.

Acknowledgments

Artists

Zella Bardsley
4621 Patton Place
Boise, ID 83704
208-378-1464
fax: 208-321-0211
e-mail: ZellaBar@aol.com

Cass Fine
Fine Creations
54 N. Midland Blvd.
Nampa, ID 83651
208-466-5702

Sheila Hudson
8604 W. High Ridge Lane
Eagle, ID 83616
208-286-7499
www.sheilahudson.net
e-mail: sheila@sheilahudson.net

James Turner
208-343-5564

Miriam Woito
2216 Longmont
Boise, ID 83706
mwoito@att.net

How-to Books

Classic Mosaic: Design and Projects Inspired by 6000 Years of Mosaic Art
By Elaine M. Goodwin

Encyclopedia of Mosaic Techniques
By Emma Biggs

Making Mosaics
By Leslie Dierks

The Mosaic Book: Ideas Projects and Techniques
By Peggy Vance and Celia Goodrick-Clarke

The Mosaic Idea Book
By Rosalind Wates

Mosaic Workshop: A Guide to Designing and Creating Mosaics
By Emma Biggs and Tessa Tankim

Mosaics: Essential Techniques and Classic Projects
By Fran Soler

Mosaics: Inspiration and Original Projects for Interiors and Exteriors
By Kaffe Fassett

Web Links

http://www.users.dircon.co.uk/~asm/mosaics/index.html
http://www.americanmosaics.org

Metric Equivalency Chart

inches to millimetres and centimetres (mm-millimetres   cm-centimetres)

inches	mm	cm	inches	cm	inches	cm	inches	cm
$1/8$	3	0.3	6	15.2	21	53.3	36	91.4
$1/4$	6	0.6	7	17.8	22	55.9	37	94.0
$3/8$	10	1.0	8	20.3	23	58.4	38	96.5
$1/2$	13	1.3	9	22.9	24	61.0	39	99.1
$5/8$	16	1.6	10	25.4	25	63.5	40	101.6
$3/4$	19	1.9	11	27.9	26	66.0	41	104.1
$7/8$	22	2.2	12	30.5	27	68.6	42	106.7
1	25	2.5	13	33.0	28	71.1	43	109.2
$1^{1}/4$	32	3.2	14	35.6	29	73.7	44	111.8
$1^{1}/2$	38	3.8	15	38.1	30	76.2	45	114.3
$1^{3}/4$	44	4.4	16	40.6	31	78.7	46	116.8
2	51	5.1	17	43.2	32	81.3	47	119.4
3	76	7.6	18	45.7	33	83.8	48	121.9
4	102	10.2	19	48.3	34	86.4	49	124.5
5	127	12.7	20	50.8	35	88.9	50	127.0

Index